Elijah

Elijah

Hearing God in the Midst of Life's Drama

SUSAN MICHELLE VAN HOOK

WestBow
PRESS
A DIVISION OF THOMAS NELSON

Unless otherwise indicated, Scripture taken from the Holy Bible, New International Version®. Copyright © 1973, 1978, 1984 Biblica. Used by permission of Zondervan. All rights reserved.

Revised Standard Version of the Bible, copyright 1952 [2nd edition, 1971] by the Division of Christian Education of the National Council of the Churches of Christ in the United States of America. Used by permission. All rights reserved.

Scripture taken from the King James Version of the Bible.

Scripture quotations are from The Holy Bible, English Standard Version® (ESV®), copyright © 2001 by Crossway, a publishing ministry of Good News Publishers. Used by permission. All rights reserved.

WestBow Press books may be ordered through booksellers or by contacting:

WestBow Press
A Division of Thomas Nelson
1663 Liberty Drive
Bloomington, IN 47403
www.westbowpress.com
1-(866) 928-1240

Because of the dynamic nature of the Internet, any web addresses or links contained in this book may have changed since publication and may no longer be valid. The views expressed in this work are solely those of the author and do not necessarily reflect the views of the publisher, and the publisher hereby disclaims any responsibility for them.

Any people depicted in stock imagery provided by Thinkstock are models, and such images are being used for illustrative purposes only.

Certain stock imagery © Thinkstock.

ISBN: 978-1-4497-2440-5 (e)
ISBN: 978-1-4497-2439-9 (sc)

Library of Congress Control Number: 2011914874

Printed in the United States of America

WestBow Press rev. date: 9/14/2011

To my husband and best friend, Brent, for loving me unconditionally and always making me laugh.

To my precious boys, Matthew and John David, for making me proud every day.

I love you!

<u>Special Thanks</u>

<u>To Sharon Mills, for all you did to help get this manuscript ready in those early days, for all the laughs and for being a wonderful friend.</u>

<u>To Joyce Williams, for believing in me, for all those edits and for being a precious mentor and friend.</u>

CONTENTS

PREVIEW IX

ACT 1: The Role of Obedience

Scene 1: Casting Call 3

Scene 2: To Obey Or Not To Obey 7

Scene 3: Trust And Obey 11

Scene 4: Attitude Adjustment 15

Scene 5: Don't Forget To Remember 18

ACT 2: Obedience Sets The Stage For Miracles

Scene 1: My Cup Overflows 25

Scene 2: Now I Know 29

Scene 3: Be Strong And Courageous 32

Scene 4: The Greatest Showdown On Earth 36

Scene 5: Point To Jesus 40

ACT 3: The Role Of Prayer

Scene 1: Sacrifice Of Praise 47

Scene 2: A Time For Prayer 51

Scene 3: The Heart Of God 54

Scene 4: Perseverant Prayer 57

Scene 5: The Hand Of God 60

ACT 4: The Role Of God's Word and Being Still

Scene 1: The Word Of God: Part 1 67

Scene 2: The Word Of God: Part 2 71

Scene 3: Too Much For You 74

Scene 4: Being Still 78

Scene 5: Speaking Of Love 82

ACT 5: A Voice From The Upperstage

Scene 1: Reality Check 89

Scene 2: Earth, Wind, And Fire! 93

Scene 3: Gentle Whispers 97

Scene 4: Enter: Elisha 100

Scene 5: The Call Of Elisha 103

ACT 6: Miscues

Scene 1: Take 1, 2, 3, 4 109

Scene 2: Naboth's Vineyard 113

Scene 3: Pride Before The Fall 118

Scene 4: Acting The Part 122

Scene 5: Curtain Call 126

DIRECTOR'S NOTES 131

ABOUT THE AUTHOR 133

CREDITS 135

PREVIEW

God still speaks today! He speaks to us through the spectacular and through the seemingly mundane. Sometimes we hear him through the voices of our children when they ask questions that cause us to stop and think. We can hear Him through the testimonies of others who experience God's grace in the midst of tragic circumstances. The Lord speaks to us through songs that touch our heart, through Scripture, and even during hilarious, everyday moments in life.

But how can we know it is the Lord speaking? How can we hear God when our lives are so busy and dominated by chaos? 1 Kings 17-2 Kings 2 is the story of the prophet Elijah and his example of how to live in tune with God's voice. Elijah's circumstances were not so different from ours. His story is full of highs and lows. He was consumed by fear for his life, depression, fatigue, and too many demands, yet, somehow, he knew His Master's voice.

Elijah's story could be translated into a dramatic, inspiring, nail-biting motion picture or an award-winning play. The story line is full of drama, laughter, and tears, and the casting in this portion of Scripture could not be more interesting—each character personified by over-the-top personalities. Therefore, we will follow Elijah's story scene by scene together. Each week of study will be referred to as an **ACT**, each day's lesson will be the next **SCENE** of Elijah's life, and I will describe the **SET** as Elijah moves from place to place. By the conclusion of our study, we will be well-versed understudies of Elijah, acutely tuned in to our Master's voice and ready for our own moments in history to play the important role God has given to each of us.

The mega theme for our study is learning to listen for the still, small voice of God. Through Elijah's example we will discover four **PREP STEPS** that play an important role in hearing God's voice:

1. Obedience
2. Prayer
3. God's Word
4. Being still

We will also use four **CRITERIA** to test if what we hear is truly from the Lord:

1. When God speaks, He will point us to Jesus.
2. When God speaks, it will be for His glory.
3. When God speaks, it will always be confirmed through His Word.
4. When God speaks, it will be in context of His love.

FORMAT

WARMING UP

The daily practice of reading God's Word is crucial for growing closer to the Lord and hearing His voice. This WARMING UP section is the Scripture reading for the lesson each day. God speaks through His Word! I encourage you to first let the Scripture passage speak to you before you read any of my words. The lessons I have written will lead you deeper, but nothing can replace the practice of daily filling your heart and mind with the Word.

ACT, SCENE

When you seek the Lord with all your heart, soul, mind, and strength, you will experience Him in deeper ways. Therefore, this level is designed for you to immerse yourself in the story five days a week, allowing God to speak through its truths and applying these truths to your life. This is when you will experience the Bible coming to life for you—alive, active, and transforming in beautiful and powerful ways! A question makes you stop and think. That is why I will ask you questions in our Bible study. Instead of only reading what I say, you will be asked to engage in the study, to discover the meaning of God's Word for yourself, and to learn to apply it to your own life. A few of the discussion questions each day are in **bold print** so that you will know which questions to discuss during your small group time. You do not have to respond out loud to all the questions unless you feel comfortable doing so. Also, make sure to have an NIV (New International Version) translation available when filling in the blanks on certain verses in our text. If you do not have an NIV, you can write the translation you have in the margin.

INTERMISSION

I cannot stress how important and vital small groups are for your study. These small groups help build healthy, godly relationships that will give you a place of belonging, encouragement, and accountability. A time of INTERMISSION is encouraged after each ACT to discuss the lessons from the previous week with your group. A leader's guide (DIRECTOR'S NOTES) is available for your convenience in the back of this book. You may also want to check out my website, susanvanhook.com, for short teaching sessions that may be viewed during your small group time or on your own.

We are given holy glimpses of our lives. We are given eyes to see the divine in the ordinary and ears to hear Him speak in the midst of our own winds, earthquakes, and fires. Will we allow God to interrupt the harried pace of our days to speak to us? Join me as we seek to recognize the Lord as He passes by in our everyday lives. If we are still, we will hear that gentle whisper that ignites a fire in our hearts.

Listen closely. He is calling.

For my Lord,
Susan Michelle

ACT 1:

THE ROLE OF OBEDIENCE

SCENE 1: CASTING CALL

SCENE 2: TO OBEY OR NOT TO OBEY

SCENE 3: TRUST AND OBEY

SCENE 4: ATTITUDE ADJUSTMENT

SCENE 5: DON'T FORGET TO REMEMBER

CASTING CALL

WARMING UP

- Begin today by asking the Holy Spirit to speak to you through His Word.
- Please read 1 Kings 16:29-33.

ACT 1, SCENE 1

Imagine this story as a motion picture or stage play. It has all the "bits" for an award-winning script: the hero; a king; the wicked queen; intriguing story lines, including a duel between one man and 850 cultic priests; stunning special effects, like fire from heaven; Elijah running faster than a chariot of horses; earthquakes, winds, and fires; a climactic moment when God whispers to Elijah; and a dramatic ending as Elijah is carried away in a chariot of fire to heaven. It even has its own theme song: "Chariots of Fire"!

As we study the life of Elijah together, I want us to immerse ourselves in the story as an audience in the front row of a play and walk scene by scene with Elijah. So grab your Bible and have a seat with me as the curtain rises . . .

THE SET:

First, we need to set the stage for our story. Let's journey back to ancient Israel. King David and King Solomon have come and gone, and now the kingdom of Israel has been divided into two separate nations: the Northern Kingdom with ten tribes (called Israel) and the Southern Kingdom with only the tribes of Judah and Benjamin (called Judah). Now we are in 876 BC. Both kingdoms have had a history of corrupt kings, who bring disastrous consequences upon the nations when they choose evil instead of worshipping God. Even most of the priests from the Tribe of Levi (the ones appointed by God to make intercession for the people of Israel) had left Israel and gone to Judah.[1]

- Have you ever been in a situation, whether at home, school, work, or the area where you live, that seemed like much of the "good" had been driven out by evil? Did you feel there was little godly atmosphere left? If so, when?

_____

_____

_____

ENTER STAGE RIGHT: KING AHAB

- **Verses 31-33 describe Ahab as one who (check all that apply):**
  ____ did more evil in the eyes of the Lord than any of those before him.
  ____ began to serve Baal and worship him after choosing to marry Jezebel.

_____ **followed the laws of God.**
_____ **built a temple for Baal in Samaria and set up an altar for him.**
_____ **set up Asherah poles.**
_____ **did more to provoke the Lord to anger than any other king of Israel before him.**
_____ **loved God and served Him faithfully.**
- **According to verse 31, whom did Ahab marry?**

_____

_____

That gives us a pretty good picture to imagine what Ahab was like: the original Dennis the Menace! It matters whom you befriend and from whom you accept advice and especially whom you marry. It affected Ahab physically, emotionally, and spiritually.

ENTER STAGE LEFT: JEZEBEL

Jezebel. Her name alone sends shivers up my spine. She was the daughter of the high priest and king of Tyre in Phoenicia, also called "king of the Sidonians" in verse 31. But this was no godly high priest. I dare say he sacrificed more than sheep, and his rituals were probably haunting. It was not uncommon for pagan priests to sacrifice their own children to their gods. Unfortunately this was the influence into which Ahab married.

- According to 1 Kings 16:34, at what cost was Jericho built during the reign of Ahab?

_____

Ahab and Jezebel worshipped the Canaanite god, Baal, and together they set up idols and altars that reflected their pursuit of power and pleasure. Ahab sacrificed his own soul when he chose to marry this pagan princess. Jezebel was very much the catalyst to Ahab's evil ways and the downfall of Israel physically and spiritually. Jezebel held great power over her husband, the cultic priests, and the people of Israel. And she was a living nightmare for anyone who defied her pagan gods. She ranks as one of the most evil women mentioned in the Bible.

- How is Jezebel described in Revelation 2:20-21?

_____

ENTER CENTER STAGE: ELIJAH

This is the Bible's first mention of Elijah. When starting this Bible study, I looked for earlier mention of Elijah, but found none. 1 Kings 17 just jumps right in, giving no extra details about Elijah's past. I don't know about you, but I like a story with lots of details, emotion, and information. So let's glean all we can about Elijah from Chapter 17, verse 1.

- "Now Elijah the _____, from _____ in _____, said . . ."

Elijah was one of a long line of important prophets God sent to Israel and Judah. The role of priest was to represent the people to God. The role of prophet was to speak for God to the people. No doubt God had something to say to Ahab and all of Israel about their rejection of the Lord and His precepts. The children of Israel were acting very rebelliously and were in need of a "holy timeout!" With the lack of godly influence from priests or kings during this period in Israel's history, God decided to bring prophets for the next three hundred years to give both Northern and Southern nations another chance.[2]

Unbelievable! Just when I would be ready to call the whole thing quits and bring justice and punishment to an idolatrous, evil, provoking people, God decides to show mercy. I will never get over it. I am so glad that He is God, aren't you? We will never fully comprehend the depth of His love for us and His unparalleled compassion, patience, and mercy!

- When someone disappoints you or hurts you, what is your likely response?
  ____ cut off the relationship

  ____ take revenge

  ____ tolerate the abuse and allow it to happen again

  ____ forgive and give him or her another chance

  ____ have difficulty trusting again

Not only did the Lord not give up on His people, He came up with a new plan to lead His people back to Him. He began to use unexpected persons with no credentials or necessary genealogy that traditionally had been required when leading the spiritual agenda of a nation (see Deut. 18:1-8). In addition to using priests, kings, and judges, now God used prophets to bring His Word to the people of Israel.

And so began the amazing story of Elijah that we have been given the privilege to observe. With so many miracles performed and the unbelievable faith and bravery of Elijah, we can be tempted to focus on his performance. But the real story is behind the scenes. If it were not for all the hard work done with his Director, he would have had nothing to offer when it came time to perform. "The real miracle in Elijah's life was his very personal relationship with God."[3]

Elijah's story can be our story. The truth is this story has all the ingredients to be a blockbuster hit for our own lives. We have enough drama of our own to fill in the subtitles. We have our own stage, our own plot, and our own characters (perhaps some very interesting characters), but the role God has invited us to play is much the same. Maybe there will be no fire from heaven, but in this time and place where God has put us, there is a great need for those who will proclaim His message of forgiveness, hope, and unbelievable mercy. Just when it seems that the darkness around us will never end, God's presence breaks through to bring light to a dark world—through us. But we must be in tune with God's voice to know what role we are to play.

- **What have you personally witnessed or heard about lately that makes it seem like the *darkness* of this world will never end? What do you wish you could do about it?**

  _____

  _____

- Write a prayer telling the Lord of your desire to seek His voice and His direction. Ask Him to reveal the part He has for you to play to bring His light to this situation:

  _____

  _____

  _____

Like all great stories, it is the opening line that grabs our attention and the closing that grabs our hearts. This story begins and ends with the same amazing scene for Elijah and for us. It is a miracle more powerful and life changing than any windstorm or fire in our story. *It is the miracle of knowing God.* From His opening lines of creation, through the masterful themes of history, to the climactic days of Revelation, God has sought to capture our attention and our hearts. No act, no scene, no words, and no bravery can change this world without first knowing God personally.

We have been invited to play a crucial role in God's plan for this world. May we commit to the challenge of being Elijah's understudy and allow God to teach us straight from the script of His Word the valuable role He has for each of us to play. This is no dress rehearsal—this is life! Everything that God offered Elijah He also offers to us: His power, His Word, and His presence. We too can make a difference in a dark world, and we can experience the miracle of knowing the Lord personally and powerfully.

Let's tune our hearts to the gentle voice of our Master as He directs each dramatic and ever-changing chapter of our lives. Miracles await us!

TO OBEY OR NOT TO OBEY

WARMING UP

- Begin today by asking the Holy Spirit to speak to you through His Word.
- Please read: 1 Kings 17:2-5; 8-10; 18:1-2; 36; 19:15-19; and 2 Kings 1:3-4; 15.
- What do these verses have in common?

_____

_____

ACT 1, SCENE 2

PREP STEP #1: OBEDIENCE

I am so glad you are on this journey with me to glean from these rich pages of 1 Kings. There is so much that God wants to teach us in these passages. I know that it is His desire for us to learn from these stories—the good, the bad, and the ugly! Today we will begin learning from Elijah's example the first of four ways we can prepare our hearts to hear the Lord more clearly in our lives. The truth is that these four steps are not well-kept secrets that I have uncovered; instead, these are actually the most basic of spiritual disciplines. The challenge is not in discovering the secrets but in how to *apply* these life-changing practices each day. And it is life changing! Preparing your heart daily to hear God speak to you personally will allow you to experience that His love is "better than life" (see Psalm 63). But because the word *discipline* makes me think more of avoiding chocolate cake and exercising on the treadmill than of spiritual blessings, we will refer to these disciplines as *preparation steps* or PREP STEPS for the remainder of our study together.

Obedience is the first PREP STEP we will cover in this series because I believe everything else we will study hinges upon this subject. We must settle this issue without going any farther until we are ready to obey what we hear God saying to us. It will do us no good to seek His voice if we do not resolve ahead of time that we will obey His commands.

- What images come to mind for you when you think of obedience?

_____

_____

When I think of obedience, I have flashbacks of times when I asked for forgiveness or times when it was my turn to forgive. Sometimes obedience, for me, means changing the channel, looking the other way, saying yes to a godly assignment, or having a more patient attitude with my kids. When we think of obedience, we might think of big tasks like accepting God's call to be a missionary to a foreign country or suddenly stopping an addictive habit. Sometimes God speaks in everyday ways and sometimes He whispers life-changing commands. But our response should always be the same. Obedience is simply depending on God to help us one day at a time . . . one choice at a time . . . sometimes one minute at a time.

- Look up Romans 7:15-20. No, Paul was not tipsy. He had a point. In your own words, how do we normally act on our own?

- According to verses 24-25, what is the key to overcoming ourselves and having power over sin?

Depending on the power of God to get me through my day is not something I do on a case-by-case basis. I can't do *anything* worthy of God's approval except through the power of the cross; therefore, I bring every temptation, task, and weakness to Jesus, asking for His strength, wisdom, and power to make it through that day or that moment. Then I do it again the next day and the next . . .

THE SET:

I know that Bible study takes time, but aren't you thankful that God allows us to learn from the mistakes of others in Scripture instead of having to figure out our problems the hard way each time? I am so glad that Israel had to go first! Unfortunately, today we will witness Israel's choice to disobey and the consequences of their sin.

One day when my son, John David, was four years old, I overheard him have a one-way conversation with our Labradoodle. Evidently, Sneaker had done something that John David did not approve of, and he felt the need to teach Sneaker some of the tough lessons of life. I heard John David say, "No, no, Sneaker. You can't do that. When you disobey, there are 'conchtaquences.'" I wish John David had been able to set Israel straight as well, but instead, Israel had to learn the hard way through their "conchtaquences."

- **According to Chapter 17, verse 1, what did Elijah prophesy to Ahab?**

- **Had Elijah's prophecy to Ahab come true in Chapter 18, verse 1?**

- **How many years of drought had Israel experienced?**

The dry, parched land was symbolic of the hardened hearts of the Israelites caused by sin and idolatrous living. God allowed the famine to become severe in the land until the hearts of those who had strayed away were ready to admit their desperate need for Him. Lord willing, we will not go that route if we allow God to show us how to recognize when the drought is setting in before a dry, cracked, and fruitless life becomes our "conchtaquences."

Now that we have witnessed the devastating consequences of disobedience for Israel, let's look at the benefits of obedience contrasted through Elijah's life:

Obedience = free flow of the Holy Spirit

Elijah went where he was told to go and did what he was told to do. No question. Therefore, the Lord continued to speak to Elijah, and Elijah continued to hear Him clearly. Allow me an analogy: Obedience is like controlling the flow of blood through our veins. Disobedience clogs the free flow of the Spirit in our lives, but obedience keeps the portals open to receive all God has for us. Just as keeping open the flow of oxygenated blood is vital to our hearts, keeping open the free flow of the Spirit is vital to our spiritual ears. The Holy Spirit speaks, but we will hear Him less and less clearly if we keep pushing Him away by disobedience. I am becoming more aware of the feeling of conviction I get when something is blocking the flow of God's voice in my life. The silence and dullness of my spirit when clogged by rebellion is excruciating compared to the passion and joy that I feel in His presence.

- Let's go no further today until all of us have had a chance to settle this issue. Take a moment right now and check your spiritual pulse. If you are not hearing God's voice clearly, ask Him to reveal any area of your life in which you may have unchecked sin or reluctance to obey when God calls to you.

Obedience = love

The surest sign of love for God is obedience. Jesus said, "If you obey my commands, you will remain in my love, just as I have obeyed my Father's commands and remain in His love" (John 15:10). Elijah was quick to obey as soon as he heard God's commands. "A slow response may be little better than disobedience."[4] We did not read of Elijah stalling God by throwing out excuses such as: "I am so busy right now with all these miracles, I just can't squeeze one more thing in," or "I can't go talk to Ahab; he has his life and I have mine. When I go home, I just want peace and quiet. I don't want to stir up trouble with my neighbors," or "That sounds dangerous; let me pray about it a little while." Thankfully, Elijah went where he was told and one miracle after another followed his obedience. He did not know what would happen next or even where his next meal would come from most of the time, but he used his obedience as his *act of worship* and love for his Lord.

- Is there anything you sense God is asking you to do? Do you have any excuses for not doing it at this time? If so, write them here:

  _____

  _____

- How can your obedience in this situation become an act of worship?

  _____

  _____

Obedience = surrender

Sneaker is lovable and cuddly and looks like a big piece of shag carpet with a tail. His personality is as laid-back as any dog's can be, but we decided to go ahead and enroll him in obedience school to make sure we knew how to control him and get the best out of this great dog. Sneaker was the star pupil in his class, if you ask me, passing each stage of training with ease and beauty. He learned to sit, stand, walk with me, play nice with other dogs, respond to commands, and do tricks. I was sure he would be valedictorian of his class. But then we hit a snag. Sneaker did not want to lie down. When I gave the command, "Down," I had to learn to step on his leash very close to his collar to force his head and body in a down position. Then the trainer explained that this was the most advanced trick for the dog to do because it is a complete surrender of his own will. It puts him in a position of vulnerability and an attitude of submission. Actually, the trainer said it is not a trick at all. It is a position that is to be used to save the dog's life. If a car was coming and the dog was on the other side of the street, it would not be safe to tell the dog to come to you. And you certainly could not let the dog continue to roam around, unleashed, at the mercy of oncoming traffic. In this instance I would call to him and yell, "Sneaker. DOWN!" The dog should immediately lie down and, therefore, not run out into the oncoming cars. It would save his life.

The word "surrender" does not have warm and fuzzy connotations in our language. Synonyms of surrender are actually "give up," "quit," "forgo," "relinquish."[5] We see visions of a white flag and defeat. Just as it was for Sneaker in obedience school, we have to learn to trust our Master. When we truly believe that He is good and loving and only wants to protect us, we can "relinquish" our control and trust Him with our lives.

- Look up Proverbs 1:33 (NIV) and fill in the blanks:
  "but whoever listens to me will live in _____ and ____ ____ _____, without _____ ___ _____."

Unfortunately, Israel did not get the message. But when we lay down our own will, even when it does not make sense, we become moldable—trainable, if you will. When we trust God and obey what He commands, we step into His will and into the center of His purpose for our lives. That is when we will see that He is not a cruel Master asking us to lie down and surrender our own will. Instead we will see that He is *giving us life*!

- Do you know Jesus personally as the One who gives you everlasting life? Have you asked Him to forgive you of all your sins? If you have not asked Jesus to be your Savior, please pray the most important prayer of your life with me right now:

  Dear Heavenly Father,
  I ask in Jesus's name that you will forgive me of all my sins. I know that I am a sinner and I need you. Jesus, I believe that you are the Son of God and that you died for my sins so I could live eternally in heaven with you. Without you, I am lost! Come into my heart today and make it your home. I will live for you in obedience according to what the Bible says is right and true from this moment forward. Thank you for giving me LIFE now and for eternity!
  In Jesus's name, Amen!

TRUST AND OBEY

WARMING UP

- Begin today by asking the Holy Spirit to speak to you through His Word.
- Please read 1 Kings 17:2-12.

ACT 1, SCENE 3

While sitting in a drive-thru recently I grimaced at the poor condition of my hands and nails. Not a big surprise since I could not remember when I last had time for a manicure. But as I turned my hands over, I found several calluses and scars on the palms of my hands that I had not noticed before. I was pretty sure that I had not done any recent hard labor—unless you count doing mounds of laundry and dirty dishes. Then I remembered: These were not recent scars. These scars were from fifteen years ago . . .

No horror stories to tell. Actually, it's about golf. When my husband and I were newlyweds, one of our favorite things to do was meet after work and play golf. But in my beginner status I held the club all wrong; I gripped it too tightly and I swung it too hard trying to force the ball where I wanted it to go. During those early years of learning to play golf I hit sand and clumps of grass farther than my ball. Forcing it did not help, but it made sense to me. You want the ball to go far, you hit it real hard! But forcing my swing and gripping the club so tightly just made things worse . . . on my score and on my hands.

Unfortunately, I learn the hard way in golf and in life. It's easy to hold on too tightly. Life is full of uncertainty, challenges, and changes. I think I know myself so well. And I think I know what is best for me, so I try to force my circumstances in the direction I think they should go.

Today we are going to look at the benefits of living a life of obedience even when it does not make sense. We can trust God when He allows our lives to take a different course than we had planned. Let's look now at the story of the Widow of Zarephath as inspiration to give all we have to God—even when it seems insignificant and confusing—and see what happens when we loosen our grip!

THE SET:

- In 1 Kings 17:4-7, where did Elijah go and how did God provide for Elijah?

_____

_____

Elijah was in hiding even though he obeyed God. God commanded Elijah to hide in the Kerith Ravine because Ahab and Jezebel did not like the message Elijah delivered. In their world, no one told Ahab and Jezebel anything they did not want to hear without deadly consequences.

I imagine the script could have read something like this:

ELIJAH: "So, Ahab, what do you want to hear first: The bad news or the bad news?"

AHAB: "Just tell me what I want to hear or I will throw a temper tantrum!"

JEZEBEL: Give my Snookums whatever he wants or I will have your head!"

Obedience is necessary to a life in tune with God, but it does not ensure an easy life. Yet, as Elijah trusted and obeyed God, he became the recipient of God's power and provisions.

God Provides through Daily Miracles:

We can be certain that if God asks us to do something, He will provide a way. God provided for Elijah through ravens to bring his food and a brook from which to drink. God provided for Elijah as he needed, but not an unlimited supply. Eventually the brook dried up. *We cannot live on yesterday's miracles*. We need a fresh encounter with God daily to meet each day's needs—physically and spiritually.

- How did God provide food for the Israelites in the desert? (Exodus 16:35)

  _____

- How long did it last?

  _____

I asked my boys after church one Sunday what they learned in Sunday school. My youngest was trying to describe the Ark of the Covenant to me because he couldn't remember what it was called. So he said, "You know, Mommy, it had the Ten Commandments in it and the jar of *mayonnaise*." I think he meant manna. Was that your answer also?

- **Lamentations 3:22-23 says, "His mercies are new_____
  _____." (Praise God!)**
- **Why do you think God often provides for us a little at a time?**

  _____

  _____

If God showed us His plan for our lives and gave us all the provisions we needed at one time, He knows we would never seek Him. We would not need to cling to Him daily. There would be no need to trust. And, saddest of all, there would be no relationship. When God provides everything we need (not want) each day, we are experiencing the tender mercies of our compassionate Heavenly Father. When we meet the Lord in a fresh, powerful, and personal way each day, we *are* experiencing a miracle!

- When have you had to trust God one day at a time? What did you learn from that experience?

  _____

  _____

  _____

<u>ENTER:</u> THE WIDOW OF ZAREPHATH

- Now that the brook dried up, where did God lead Elijah in 1 Kings 17:10?

_____

- What did Elijah ask of the widow in verses 10-11?

_____

- What was the widow's response in verse 12?

_____

Sometimes life just doesn't make sense. God sent Elijah to a woman that was not even an Israelite and then asked the widow to give up everything. It was a huge sacrifice for the widow of Zarephath to give the last of her food to Elijah—especially when she did not know God personally. But she had heard of the God of Elijah and was willing to take a chance. Knowing that this woman was a widow tells us that this was not the first time her life took a detour. I am sure that when she was a little girl this was not the life that she dreamed of having some day. But God specializes in taking our helplessness and turning it into hope!

Sometimes obedience is a sacrifice, and God asks us to trust Him even when we are not given any additional explanation. Times of change, pain, sorrow, and sacrifice can cause us to question God's plan and His provisions. Suffering can even cause us to doubt His presence. But our obedience in times of sacrifice allows us a chance to see the miracles of God! Our own lives become a testimony of God's glory, His goodness, and living proof that He is enough!

- Now read verse 15. What happened to the oil and flour?

_____

_____

Hear the good news: God's power and provisions are never used up and our cups will never run dry when we trust in Him! Like the widow, we learn that God gives us grace for each moment of need when we offer Him the little remnant of oil and flour in our jar. Sometimes He gives back to us in full measure; and sometimes He gives just enough for the moment. But that is when we learn that HE is enough for every circumstance. The Lord gives us encouragement when we are brokenhearted, rest when we are weary, provisions for our needs, healing for our bodies, forgiveness for our sins, and wisdom for our days right when we need it. We can afford to give what the Lord asks of us—even if it doesn't seem possible—because we serve a God who does the impossible . . . for us!

Even now as I look down at my scarred hands I hear God's gentle whisper in my ears. "Let go," He says, as I wrestle with understanding the direction He is taking my family. _Let go_ of the frazzled lifestyle and insane amount of to-do's on my list. _Let go_ of micromanaging my children and let them blossom on their own, even if that involves a few mistakes along the way. _Let go_ of micromanaging my own life in the way I think it should go and allow God the chance to surprise me once in a while.

- **I am pretty sure I am not alone in my golf cart. How is God gently whispering to you about letting go? Is there some area of your life in which you are holding on too tightly?**

_____

_____

I am a slow learner. But I finally learned how to play golf. It's all in the grip. Loosen your grip, relax your swing, and listen to the ball hit the sweet spot—well, sometimes. The result is a long, straight shot that lands the ball right where it should go (okay, just take my word for it!) I am learning how to loosen my grip in life as well. The key is letting go. More trusting. Less trying so hard. Even in uncertainty, I can trust that God is good, that He loves me, and that He knows the best course for my life.

We can afford to give God whatever He asks of us—tithes, offerings, time, talents, our future, our family—because when we place these things that He has given to us back into His hands, He will miraculously and faithfully multiply them. And, like the Widow of Zarephath, we will stand back amazed as God does "immeasurably more than all we ask or imagine according to His power at work within us" (Eph. 3:20)!

ATTITUDE ADJUSTMENT

WARMING UP

- Begin today by asking the Holy Spirit to speak to you through His Word.
- Please read 1 Kings 17:11-15 and Mark 12:41-44.

ACT 1, SCENE 4

Are you ready to hear from the Lord today? I believe God has a special lesson for us. I know this because He has already used it to speak straight to my heart and help me make some needed adjustments in my life. Just when I thought I had the issue of obedience settled with God, He put His finger on another area in my life that I had not seen. Thankfully, through experience, I have learned that it is definitely worth it to *go there* with God when He gently nudges me toward greater obedience. For it is at these times that He is simply molding me into the image of His Son, Jesus Christ. And that is definitely worth it! So, are you ready to *go there* with me and see what type of makeover God may want to do in you to make you into His image? If so, then let's put on our sandals and pick up where we left off on our journey with Elijah.

THE SET:

- What did the Widow of Zarephath do in verse 15 when Elijah asked for her last meal?

  _____

  _____

- The Widow of Zarephath reminds me of another widow in Mark 12:41-44 (Also recorded in Luke 21:1-4). What similarities do you see in these two stories?

  _____

  _____

There is no right or wrong answer. God uses His Word to speak to each of us in very personal ways. Hallelujah! Both women gave such sacrificial gifts. Yet, what spoke to me personally were their attitudes. No one forced them to give all they had. These two widows gave not knowing the outcome. They gave *everything*, not to receive, but from hearts of trust and gratitude. To give everything we have with joy and without reluctance is a different level of obedience than merely obeying God.

- **What did Jesus say about the widow's gift in Mark 12:43?**

  _____

  _____

This is where God started speaking to me personally and called me to a deeper walk of obedience . . .

My husband and I were in the midst of a transition in our ministry that required acts of faith and obedience on our part. Being confident of God's will, we chose to follow His lead and made the necessary changes. But I did not realize that my feet were moving, but my heart was stuck. Then, after hearing a sermon about the widow giving all she had in Mark 12, I felt the voice of God speak to me deep in my soul. He said, "Susan, it is the same with any type of obedience—not just financial giving. I don't want you to just go through the motions just to say you did it. I want all of you. I want your heart to be in it, not just your hands and feet. I want you to give me your obedience in this area of your life *with joy* as your act of worship to me."

And as Emeril says, "BAM!" Right between the eyes and straight to my heart!

- How does Psalm 100:2 say we should serve (some translations say "worship") the Lord?

_____

_____

To bring a pleasing offering to the Lord is to serve Him with a good attitude. Our acts of obedience with joy and gladness *are* our offerings of worship to God. It is out of a heart of thankfulness for His overwhelming goodness to us that we give our joyful obedience to Him in whatever way He asks—staying, going, giving, adding, serving, stopping, starting—you fill in the verb. But one thing is the same for all of us: God desires our *hearts* more than anything else. Obviously doing the right thing still matters; it is obedience we are talking about after all. But the wrong attitude can still trump the right action. Our obedience becomes little better than lip service, like the Pharisees, unless we give with all our hearts!

- Is there anything you are presently doing or feel He is asking you to do that may require an attitude adjustment on your part as you obey?

_____

_____

When I was a physician assistant student I decided to go to Africa for my OB/GYN medical rotation for six weeks. So as a twenty-one-year-old, I went by myself to the other side of the world with great excitement and anticipation of all I was going to experience. (And I left my parents behind on their knees in prayer!) But when I finally arrived in Africa, I froze. I began to worry that the reason God planted the idea in my heart to go to Africa was so that He could get me there and then call me to be a missionary. All of the sudden all the joy of my trip drained out of me and I spent weeks fretting over my future. Then one day I talked with a missionary about my worries and she said one of the most liberating statements of my life. She said, "Oh, Susan, don't worry. Because when you are in God's will, you will have JOY!" That was music to my ears and comfort for my soul. I was so relieved because I DIDN'T HAVE JOY!

I say that jokingly, but, seriously, that was when God released me from my worries and taught me a valuable lesson in seeking His will for my life. Since that time, I have been called into full-time ministry with my husband, and I have SO MUCH JOY! When I said "yes" to God's call on my life, He gave me supernatural joy. I am not saying that we should go do whatever makes us happy and that means that we are in God's will. We are commanded to be faithful with what God has given us to do right where He has placed us. When we seek God's will through prayer and His

Word, He will be faithful to show us the right way to go. And He will bless our obedience and give us a supernatural joy as we complete our task.

The best example of this is not the widow or even Elijah, but Jesus Christ.

- **Please read Hebrews 12:2. Why did Jesus endure the cross and scorn its shame? (Fill in the blanks) "Who ___ ___ ___ set before him . . . " (NIV).**

The perfect Lamb of God who asked for "this cup to be taken from me" (Matt. 26:39), obediently and *joyfully* gave all He had. How was that possible?

Because Jesus was smack-dab in the center of His Father's will!

Our joy in serving the Lord comes from knowing that we are in the center of His will. We can be assured of that joy, no matter how high the cost, because Jesus showed us that joy can be found when our eyes are firmly set on the Father! I pray that God's words to each of us during this lesson have melted our hearts if there were any issues that had us *stuck* in a place of un-joyful obedience. When we feel God's call to go to a deeper level of obedience, remember that we are tenderly being molded into the likeness of Jesus. I am on the potter's wheel with you, dear one. This extreme makeover He is doing on us will be worth all the effort when we emerge reflecting the image of God's precious Son!

- Please look up 2 Corinthians 3:18 and write it in your own words here:

  _____

  _____

  _____

Won't you join me in serving the Lord with gladness? Let's make our every act of obedience our offering of joyful worship to the One who is so worthy!

DON'T FORGET TO REMEMBER

WARMING UP

- Begin today by asking the Holy Spirit to speak to you through His Word.
- Please read 1 Kings 17:17-20.

ACT 1, SCENE 5

This past week we focused on our first PREP STEP: OBEDIENCE. And we learned that we can afford to obediently go when God asks us to go, stay when He asks us to stay, give what He asks us to give, and trust when God asks us to wait. But how is that possible? What is the secret to living a life that trusts God so confidently that we can walk on the wild side of faith? *Our memory!*

When the men in my house can't remember where they left something, I seem to know exactly where I last saw it. I think it is the spiritual gifting of women to know right where to find lost games, retainers, library books, teddy bears, and missing tennis shoes. So why can't I ever seem to remember why I went into a room for something?

I am in good company. Elijah and the Widow of Zarephath also had memory problems. God provided for Elijah's needs over and over. God was faithful to the widow when the oil and flour in the jar was not used up. But when the widow's son was dying, they both seemed to quickly forget God's faithfulness.

- Look at verses 18-20. Who did the widow blame for her son's illness? Who did Elijah blame?

_____

_____

In addition to the boy's illness, it seems there was also a serious epidemic of *amnesia* going around!! Elijah and the widow developed Spiritual Amnesia when they *forgot to remember* God's faithfulness in the past. When we forget how much has God done for us, we begin to worry about the future and complain about our present circumstances. Unfortunately, these are the symptoms when we develop the disease of Spiritual Amnesia.

- **Please read Matthew 6:25-34. Why does God tell us not to worry?**

_____

_____

_____

- **What are some symptoms we may notice when worry creeps into our lives?**

_____

_____

_____

God knows that worry may kill us before our problems do! What, then, is the cure for our Spiritual Amnesia and the antidote for worry? The treatment is, obviously, *to remember.*

1. REMEMBER . . . GOD'S FAITHFULNESS!

It is too easy to let our present circumstances rob us of our memory of God's faithfulness to us in the past. We forget all God has brought us through in the past and fail to apply these memories to our present needs.

My temptation to worry usually involves my children. I am tempted to worry about their health, forgetting that God has brought them this far. I worry about their social and school issues, forgetting that God is with them now just as He always has been in the past. And I sometimes worry about what would happen to them if something happened to my husband or me, even though God has always been faithful.

- Does this ever happen to you? When do fear and worry get a hold on you?

_____

_____

We must not let FEAR of the future rob us of the TRUTH of our past!

When I was four years old, my mom died of leukemia, leaving behind my dad and three children between the ages of four and eleven. Was it easy for me after losing my mom at such a young age? Of course not. Do I still struggle at times with my loss? Sure. But I can testify to God's grace in times of heartache. God sent special family and friends into my life to care for me. And, most importantly, I always sensed that God's hand was upon me. I was given a joy that permeated my life despite my circumstances!

So, what I must remember is: Why would it be any different for my children during the difficult circumstances they may face during their lives? God will be faithful to them just as He has been to me. And why would that be any different for you?

- **Can you think of a time when God was faithful to you even in the midst of tough circumstances? Did He send someone to help carry your burden? Did He provide for you in some way?**

_____

_____

Now think for a minute about what you or those you love may presently be facing. Apply God's faithfulness in the past to your present needs. Rehearse His faithfulness by reading the Bible and remembering how God kept His promises to His children throughout the ages. Apply those promises to your life. He will be with you today just as before. He will provide for your needs once again. And best of all, His presence can bring you joy that permeates even your most difficult circumstances.

The next cure for Spiritual Amnesia is:

2. REMEMBER . . . TO PRAY.

Prayer itself is the antidote for worry. *The peace that comes from prayer is part of God's faithfulness to us.* When we place our cares in the hands of our caring God, the burden is released even before the problem is fixed. We are reminded of God's power, HIS ability to care for us, and we are comforted.

- Elijah got his faith back on track in verse 21. What did Elijah do?

  _____

  _____

Although Elijah probably should not have blamed God for the child's illness, verse 20 shows us that it is okay to cry out to God in honest prayer. We do not always understand why something difficult may be happening to those we love, but what we do know is that God is gracious, compassionate, and loving, according to Exodus 34:6-7. We may reverently approach God in prayer with our questions, but we should never question God. We can ask Him anything, but in the midst of our brokenness we should not forget to remember who He is.

Does hardship make you question God or His love for you? _____. If so, reverently cry out to God in prayer for your needs right now. Ask Him to reveal Himself to you even if you don't understand your situation.

3. REMEMBER . . . THE LORD HEARS!

Look up the following verses. Who cried out? What was God's response? And how was the individual or the situation changed?

- Exodus 6:5; 6; 7:

  _____

  _____

  _____

- John 11:33; 35; 44:

  _____

  _____

  _____

- Psalms 30:11-12:

  _____

  _____

  _____

- Genesis 16:7; 9; 10; 13:

  _____

  _____

  _____

- 1 Kings 17:20-23:

  _____

  _____

  _____

We are promised that the Lord hears us when we cry out to Him. And when God hears us—things happen! God does not sit passively by watching our pain. He gets busy! Prayers are answered, chains are broken, hearts are mended, dead cells come back to life, and hopeless souls find the hope of the Savior! If we truly know God has heard us, we have a faith-shot in the arm. Believe that things are about to change!

> The boy's life was returned to him and, "Elijah picked up the child and carried him down from the room into the house. He gave him to his mother and said, 'Look, your son is alive!'" (verse 23).

The Widow of Zarephath entered her home that day as a widow full of hurts, fears, and sorrows. But she emerged after an encounter with the God of Elijah with hope and healing and a new faith of her own. Her son received life, but she found the One who gives eternal life.

God may choose to answer your prayers just as you asked Him to. And if He does, praise Him for His faithfulness. But if the answers are different than you expect, still praise Him for His faithfulness—because you will be given something even better . . . you are given Jesus. Instead of instant healing, you will receive grace. Instead of fear and worry, you will have hope. Instead of changed circumstances, *you* will be changed! And you will find that Jesus is the best answer to your prayers that you could ever receive!

ACT 2

OBEDIENCE SETS THE STAGE FOR MIRACLES

SCENE 1: MY CUP OVERFLOWS

SCENE 2: NOW I KNOW

SCENE 3: BE STRONG AND COURAGEOUS

SCENE 4: THE GREATEST SHOWDOWN ON EARTH

SCENE 5: POINT TO JESUS

MY CUP OVERFLOWS

WARMING UP

- Begin today by asking the Holy Spirit to speak to you through His Word.
- Please read 1 Kings 17:12-16 as a reminder of today's text.

ACT 2, SCENE 1

Last week Elijah demonstrated for us the role that obedience plays in clearing the cobwebs of sin that block God's voice from being heard in our lives. We watched as each scene unfolded as if onstage right in front of us as Elijah bravely confronted the evil ways of King Ahab and Jezebel. And we witnessed the Widow of Zarephath personally experience the power of God for perhaps the first time in her life when she stepped out in faith and obedience.

This week, with the issue of obedience hopefully settled for all of us, we will charge forward to see how quickly a life lived in obedience sets the stage for miracles in our lives. Obedience opens our ears to hear God's voice, but it also produces fertile soil for blessings and miracles to grow!

We are not finished with the story of the Widow of Zarephath just yet. There are so many wonderful applications we can make for the imagery of the oil and flour in the widow's jar. Today we will deliberately focus our lens on the special effects that God can do when we obediently place our lives in His hands.

1. **Our "oil and flour" multiply when placed in God's hands:**

   - According to verse 12, how much food did the widow have to share?

   _____

   _____

The widow did not have much to offer . . . just a handful of flour and a little oil. Relying on her own strength and resources, the widow did not even have enough to provide for herself, much less to help anyone else.

   - What things are you trying to do that you cannot do on your own? When do you feel your resources limit how you would like to serve God?

   _____

   _____

God has called me to write this Bible study and what a privilege it has been! But I know that it is a task that is much bigger than me. I know my limitations. Yet, when I step out in faith and offer the Lord the handful of flour in my jar and the little bit of oil in my jug, God is able to do great things through me for His glory.

- According to Matthew 21:19, what will happen if we do not use what we are given to serve the Lord?

  _____

  _____

- In verse 15, what happened when the widow gave all she had to the Lord?

  _____

All we may see in ourselves is barely enough skill, talent, or resources to help ourselves, but just a little is all God needs. It may not seem to you like you have much to offer sometimes, but wherever God has placed you (as a mother, a spouse, in your job, in your church, in your community), that is where He wants to use you! Creating an atmosphere in your home that honors God may be hard when you are exhausted or stressed or do not have spiritual support from your spouse. But when you commit your attitudes, time, and talents to God, that is all He needs to begin a miracle in your home. The same goes for your workplace and in your church. When you offer Him ALL you have, God multiplies your gifts to make a difference through you in ways you could have never imagined.

- **What are your spiritual gifts if you know them?**

  _____

- **If you are not sure, what talents or abilities do you have? What do you enjoy doing?**

  _____

  _____

- **Are you giving these resources back to God? Are you willing to step out in faith and use these gifts—even in a small way—to serve the Lord?**

  _____

  _____

2. <u>Only God can fill our spiritual jars:</u>

God has equipped each one of us to do a special work for Him. We are given everything we need, one step at a time, to fulfill His great purpose for our lives. But it really has nothing to do with us except our willingness to be a vessel through which God can pour out His blessings. We *are* the jars of clay into which God pours the oil (See 2 Cor. 4:7). But we must continually fill ourselves up with His presence before our jars will begin to overflow.

- We are all needy, wouldn't you say? What are we using to fill the voids we have in our lives if we are not filling up with God first?

  _____

  _____

Only God can fill our jars of need. Anything else leaves us wanting and wasting away, just as the widow was experiencing *before* she met the God of Elijah. We can try to fill our jars with food, intimacy, attention, shopping (ouch!), substance abuse, and even watching too much television. Do any of these ring true for you? Dear friends, God wants to fill us up with His presence to bring us joy, contentment, purpose in life, and fullness of life. Anything else only creates an insatiable appetite that is never quenched. But the Lord fills us to overflowing!

- According to Psalm 23:5, how do our cups overflow? What does this verse mean to you?

_____

_____

- **Please look up Ephesians 3:18-19. What do we need to KNOW in order to be filled with all the fullness of God?**

_____

_____

- Write a prayer here expressing your desire to seek God and for Him to fill your cup:

_____

_____

_____

3. <u>We find purpose and significance when our spiritual jars are filled:</u>

I must admit that I sometimes struggle with believing that I am special just being me—dirty patches on my knees from gardening, in my everyday clothes, with frazzled hair from running the kids to ball practice. My picture in the back of this book would have been more accurate if I were wearing a ponytail and sweatpants! How is that special? How am I fulfilling my passion to share God's Word and change the world for Christ when I am doing the laundry?

- Do you ever feel that way?

_____

We might have dreams of making a huge difference in the world for Christ, but we might not see that happening in our ordinary, everyday life. But who is to say that the Maker of our dreams is not completing them in us even now? Right where we are. In the office, in the laundry room, in the carpool, in the choir, in the Sunday school class . . .

Recently I visited my sister's church for Vacation Bible School and decided to sit in on the class she was teaching full of energetic and bright-eyed four-year-olds. I watched as she called each child up one by one and I saw their little eyes twinkle in amazement that she knew their name. I could see the Bible story come to life for them as they realized that they were each special, chosen, and important. As I sat there in the little classroom of children who had just received and understood that Jesus loved each one of them personally, I overheard God whisper to my sister, "Well done!" And I wept because it took a room of four-year-olds and the significance of my sister's sweet ministry to help me see that each one of us is making a difference, no matter how the Lord chooses to use us. Ponytails, sweatpants, and all!

Elijah must have felt the same way at times: Wondering how God could possibly use him to reach the lost when he was hiding instead of healing, and running instead of preaching. Yet he made a difference *one life at a time* and *one day at a time* as He followed the Lord's lead. As show-stopping as Elijah's story may sound, the truth is that, for the most part, he had a very everyday type ministry. He used whatever situation he was in to make a difference in that moment. Elijah did not have to go to grad school or have a huge Internet following to be of valuable service to the Lord.

Do you realize that your life is valuable? Your value can't be measured by how *successful* you may or may not feel at the moment. Instead fix your eyes on the One who created you as His masterpiece, and suddenly your worth will come from who *He* thinks you are. And He thinks you are a treasure—no matter how frazzled your hair may be. Just keep your cup overflowing with His presence and you will hear His voice leading you to a special plan that only you were created to do. You can make a difference . . . just by being YOU!

Then listen closely as your Father gently whispers, "Well done, good and faithful servant" (Matthew 25:23a)!

NOW I KNOW

WARMING UP

- Begin today by asking the Holy Spirit to speak to you through His Word.
- Please read 1 Kings 17:12; 17-24.

ACT 2, SCENE 2

There are so many rich truths for us in these pages of God's Word! Deuteronomy 32:47 says God's words "are not just idle words for you—they are your life!" I love doing LIFE with you! In the past few days we have spent quite a bit of time on Chapter 17 because there has been a lot to unpack in these verses. Believe it or not, much material fell to the cutting room floor that did not make it into the script. But we are not done quite yet. In fact, as we conclude our look at this chapter today, I believe we will be looking at one of the most important miracles that God can do through us as we obediently follow Him: When we are used by God to share the good news of Jesus Christ with others!

God used Elijah to show the Widow of Zarephath that He cared for her every need. It is the most important thing we can ever do for someone else when we share the gospel with them, but sometimes we have to take care of the needs of others before they are ready to accept our words.

- **What did the widow call the Lord when she first met Elijah in verse 12? "As surely as the LORD _____ God lives . . ." (NIV).**
- Please look up Luke 4:24-26. What was Jesus's explanation for Elijah being sent to this pagan widow instead of an Israelite?

_____

_____

This widow was from Zarephath, the territory of Jezebel. She was a widow with no hope from a people of no hope and no true God. Why should she help Elijah? More importantly, why should she *believe* in the God of Elijah? Because she was primed and ready! Her needs had been met physically and now her heart was ready to accept the one true God that seemed to care for her. She saw Elijah's faith and God's miracles through him and it changed her life forever.

Now for my favorite part of this chapter and maybe even my favorite part of Elijah's story . . .

- **After experiencing the Lord personally as He met her needs for food and saving the life of her son, what did the widow say about the Lord in verse 24? (fill in the blanks):**

"Now _____ _____ that you are a man of God and that the word of the LORD from your mouth is the truth" (NIV).

- **Look up John 4:39-42, Psalms. 20:6, and Job 42:5. What similar words were used in these verses? What happened to change the minds and hearts of these people?**

The widow's life had a new beginning and her story had a new ending because she could say, *"Now I know"* Him! Elijah's God became *her* God! Likewise, the lives of the disciples, David, and Job were changed forever when they experienced God personally in their own lives and then believed on His name.

Has your life been changed by KNOWING the God of Elijah? Can you say, "Now I know Him"? Have you seen the Lord shining through someone's life and you want what they have? *When we first seek this type of life-changing relationship with the Lord for ourselves, then we can become the light of God shining in the darkness and others will want what we have.*

At one of the churches where my husband was pastor there was a very active motorcycle ministry that was on fire for Jesus! They held small group ministries at church and in their homes, went on "rides" together, and witnessed to the life-changing power of Christ in their lives to anyone they would meet—no matter how rough around the edges. One particular man (who we will call T. Dub) was part of this group and had a contagious love for the Lord. One day he shared his faith with some bikers at an ABATE group meeting (a neutral site where bikers of every origin could come and discuss motorcycle legislations). He told them that he believed God would give him a Harley-Davidson. He needed to have a Harley in order to be accepted as a part of this group so that he could be able to minister to them. Then about four months later God did, indeed, provide him with a Harley and he shared about God's faithfulness with these non-Christian bikers. One the way home from the meeting, our friend noticed a biker chasing him down the road on a rural highway. Realizing that he could not outride him, T. Dub decided to go ahead and pull over and brace himself for what was to come. The other biker jumped off his bike and T. Dub recognized that he was a biker from the meeting he had just left. The biker (who we will call John) was a particularly rough-around-the-edges kind of guy. He came toward T. Dub and shouted, "Hey! I want what you got!" T. Dub's first thought was that John wanted to take his new Harley-Davidson. But to T. Dub's surprise, John said again, "No. I want what you got . . . here," as he pointed to his heart. Right there on the side of the road T. Dub began to lead him to the Lord. Soon afterward John began not only attending the biker small group at church, but also Sunday morning services—leather pants, tattoos, do-rags, and all. His wife was also into substance abuse and a sinful lifestyle, but we began to see her more and more frequently in church until one day she also accepted Christ as her personal Lord and Savior and her life began to change dramatically.[6]

Because of Elijah's obedience to God and his willingness to share the good news of his Lord with the widow, she and her entire household were saved! Because of the testimony of T. Dub and his obedience to share the secret of his joy and freedom with others, John's whole household was saved! Because of someone's testimony to you, you were saved! Are you changing the lives of those around you? Do you have something contagious going on with Jesus that will cause others to say, "I want what you've got!"?

- **What can keep you from sharing your faith?**

  _____

  _____

- Who has the Lord put in your life to whom you are a witness?

  _____

  _____

- Pray right now that God will give you the courage and the wisdom you need to help bring those around you to a personal relationship with Jesus.

When you have personally experienced the voice of God in your own life, you can't *not* share Him with others . . . it's just too exciting! *When you exude a contagious belief in your Lord and Savior, Jesus Christ, you are positioned to make a difference in this world!* Elijah was a prophet. T. Dub was a fairly new Christian. You may or may not be a "seasoned" Christian. But we each have our own unique story to share of how Jesus made all the difference in our lives. And that, my friend, is what it's all about! You were created for your own life-changing, personal relationship with the Lord and you were gifted in a unique way to bring others to Jesus. It may surprise you whom the Holy Spirit has primed and ready to receive God's love through you.

Our lives can be a daily testimony to those around us of God's love for them. Obedience "sets the stage" for miracles . . . the greatest of which is when your life causes someone to say, *"Now I know the Lord!"*

BE STRONG AND COURAGEOUS

WARMING UP

- Begin today by asking the Holy Spirit to speak to you through His Word.
- Please read 1 Kings 18:3-15.

ACT 2, SCENE 3

THE SET:

Imagine a hypothetical scenario with me: Suppose the president of the United States lived a life in total defiance of God and His laws. Imagine that he practiced cultic forms of worship and built shrines in which these practices were not only legal, but mandatory. Blatant public sexual immorality and sacrifice that often included the sacrifice of children were common rituals in these shrines. The practices that were previously known as *occult* became known as *freedom of worship*. In fact, anyone who tried to fight the president on these issues was put to death at the command of the first lady.

Now under the very same roof of the White House is the chief of staff, running the household as usual, yet living a secret life of his own. He is a believer. He is a worshiper of God Almighty. No one knows—no one suspects—that this servant who takes care of all the personal needs of the President would have a mind and agenda of his own. Secretly he has been hiding ministers of God and risking his own life in doing so. If found out, the headlines could soon read: INSUBORDINATION! . . . TREASON! . . . SECRET LIFE AND LIES OF WHITE HOUSE CHIEF OF STAFF!

Unfortunately this is not a fictional story. Today we will shift the spotlight from Elijah and focus our lens on a new character, Obadiah. The set changes before us to a different stage; a behind-the-scenes look at what is going on in the palace of Ahab and Jezebel.

ENTER BACKSTAGE: OBADIAH

According to Biblical timelines, this does not appear to be the same person as the prophet who wrote the book of Obadiah, but the obscure character in our story today is a hero nonetheless. The introduction of Obadiah in 1 Kings 18 proves that you do not have to be front and center to make a tremendous impact in God's kingdom. In fact, we will see that most victory happens behind the scenes.

In our current society the hypothetical scenario above seems (a little) far-fetched, but flash back a few thousand years to the life of Obadiah. This story *is* Obadiah's life. As head of Ahab's household, Obadiah saw and heard more than his fair share of corrupt politics. And he had witnessed one too many executions of godly prophets at the hands of Queen Jezebel. Somewhere along the way, this man whose name means "servant (or worshipper) of the Lord" made the choice to worship the Lord Almighty, the only True God.[7] And somewhere along the way, he had seen enough and decided to make a difference. He chose courage!

Refer to verse 4 to help answer the questions below:

- How many prophets did Obadiah hide in caves?

  _____

- How did he provide for them?

  _____

It was risky to hide these prophets, yet Obadiah continually risked his life by bringing enough food and water to feed one hundred people on a regular basis. Where did all this bread and water come from during the drought and famine? I have no trouble believing that the God who provided an endless supply of oil and flour for the widow was also working miracles in the life of His faithful servant, Obadiah.

- What have you seen enough of? What do you wish would change in this world or even in *your world* right around you?

  _____

- **What has God commanded of us numerous times in Scripture when we are faced with a difficult, even scary, task? (Refer to Joshua 1:9 for your answer.)**

  _____

  _____

We want to make a difference. We want to change the world. We sometimes just want to have enough courage to face our own day. *And we can!* But we must be strong and courageous and brave! In his book, *Just Courage,* International Justice Ministries president and CEO, Gary Haugen, says, "Who has been overcome by darkness and is having a hard time believing that God is good? *Go there!* It's not by sheer will that we have become brave. It takes reformation of the heart. God doesn't call us to *try* to be brave but to *train* to be brave."[8]

- Look again at Joshua 1:9b. What is the key to our courage?

  _____

In today's passage from 1 Kings 18, the drought had become so severe that King Ahab himself went on a search for more water. He also sent Obadiah to scout the land for fresh water. But instead of finding water, Obadiah found the infamous prophet Elijah walking toward him. Ahab had combed the countryside looking for Elijah and seeking revenge. Now Elijah requested to see Ahab. But Elijah had a funny way of disappearing when the Spirit moved him, so Obadiah was skeptical.

This dialogue between Obadiah and Elijah in verses 7-15 is almost comical. In the New King James Version, Obadiah says with emphasis the word "here" four times during these verses. Here's my translation:

"You mean you want me to say to Ahab, 'Elijah is *here*', but we have been looking *here* for three years. If I say you are *here* and then you're not *here*, he's gonna kill me right *here*! Haven't you heard about all I've already done for God's prophets around *here*, and now you want me to risk my neck for you too?! *Here* we go again!"

- **Do you ever feel like even when you do the right thing and are obedient to God, it seems like things just aren't working out? If so, when?**

_____

_____

Life feels that way sometimes! You follow the rules, you labor and serve and sacrifice, but it still seems like the enemy is winning the battle. It is tempting to say, "You mean I sacrificed for this?" Sometimes the daily battles get overwhelming, don't they? You serve the Lord faithfully, yet life doesn't always go the way you planned. Your spouse gets cancer, ends don't meet each month, you endure a thankless job, you have enemies even though you try to do the right thing, or you wonder if your children will be the death of you.

It is easy to think that when we sign up for the Jesus team, things should go smoothly for us, and we may forget Jesus's words to "take up your cross daily and follow me" (Luke 9:23). Obedience is not always easy—or even safe. But we have been called to stay faithful and join the fight even when it gets tough, because there is more to our battle than meets the eye.

When my son, John David, was four years old, he loved superhero cartoons. Obsessed was more like it. He mimicked their every move, he wore their costumes, he talked about their shows, and he sang their theme songs. It is partly just being a boy. Boys love to fight and they especially love to win. But it is also just being human. Every good book, movie, and bedtime story has a plot decorated with the scenes of an evil villain or the selfish desires of a rival, which have taught us since childhood of the seen and unseen powers that seek to destroy us. But we all know that most of these stories will have a happy ending.

Our own true stories are filled with some scary battles and even a few touch-and-go moments, but we can be certain of a triumphant ending too! We have already peeked at the last chapter and know "who-dun-it" and how the story will end. It ends in victory for the children of the Lord, but we still must stand up and fight until the end. Again quoting from Gary Haugen's book, *Just Courage*, "While the Bible does not teach that we will prevail in every battle against injustice on this earth, it does teach us that God will prevail in the ultimate war, that he goes with us into every battle, that he brings his power and protection to bear on our behalf, and that he will prevail in all battles necessary to the ultimate triumph of his kingdom."[9]

- In John 17:13-15, for whom did Jesus pray?

_____

_____

_____

- What was Jesus's request?

_____

Jesus is for us! We know Somebody who knows Somebody, and He is assuredly pulling some strings for us behind the scenes. We may feel like we are on the front line sometimes, but we are not left to fight alone. In 2 Kings 6:8-23, Elisha prayed that the eyes of his frightened servant be opened. Then his servant saw the unseen: Hills full of horses and chariots of fire all around Elisha. Elisha said to him, "Those who are for us are more than those who are with them."

The battle is not ours—the battle is HIS! All the greatest work is being done in the *upper stage* on our behalf and for His glory! When we are afraid or overwhelmed, we can afford to be brave and obediently take a stand, because the Lord fights for us! Obadiah became a quiet hero because of his bravery and obedience. He was used by God to save the lives of many people around him. Yet he needed to be reminded once again that everything would be okay, even when the scene looked bleak around him. Obadiah had no need to worry, because God was about to show up and put an end to all doubts of who was in control!

Stay faithful, dear friend, and hold fast to the hope of victory. God is working behind the scenes. He is in control. And he is about to do yet another miracle . . . for you!

See you tomorrow. I can't wait!

THE GREATEST SHOWDOWN ON EARTH

WARMING UP

- Begin today by asking the Holy Spirit to speak to you through His Word.
- Please read 1 Kings 18:19-39.

ACT 2, SCENE 4

THE SET:

- According to verse 20, where is Elijah now?

_____

The backdrop for today's story changes dramatically as we begin the ascent up Mount Carmel for one of the most famous showdowns in history. So that we don't miss one exciting detail in this story, we will break down our scripture passage today like stepping-stones as we climb the mountain together.

1. Do the math (verses 19-20):

- In verse 19, how many prophets of Baal were present?

_____

- How many prophets of Asherah? _____. So how many prophets total?

_____

- If this were a math equation, what would be the correct answer? **(<, >, or =)**

    850 cultic prophets _____ Elijah + GOD

With God ALL things are possible (Luke 1:37). Numerous stories in the Bible recount the faithfulness of God to bring victory to His saints when it seemed the odds were against them. This was the case for Gideon, Joshua, Moses, David, and Elijah, just to name a few. And it is true for us also. Many times it may seem that our strength is limited and no one else is on our side, yet when we rely on the power of God to see us through, there is victory! Do you need that reminder today? I know I do! God loves a chance to show up and show off His glory. And His glory shines brightest when we are weakest, for "when we are weak then we are strong." (See 2 Corinthians 12:10.) Sometimes our limited perspective leads us to believe that our situation is hopeless, but God wants the world to see that He is a God of miracles. So let's do the math in our own lives:

- What circumstances are you facing that seem too big for you to handle on your own?

  _____

  _____

- **Now fill in the blanks:** _____ < _____ **+ GOD**

  (your problem)   **(your name)**

The journey up Mount Carmel might have been ominous for Elijah, but he believed God was sovereign over any earthly equation. Nothing and no one can stand against us when we are on God's side of the equation. With the God of Elijah, the enemy is always outnumbered! Let's climb our own Mount Carmels with faith and get ready to see a showdown of magnificent proportions unfold before our eyes!

2. <u>Another case of memory loss (verses 21-24):</u>

It was tradition for Israelite families to pass down stories of God's faithfulness and deliverance from one generation to the next (Exodus 13:8; Joshua 4:6-7). Songs and stories of God's miracles in their behalf were as common as lullabies and bedtime stories are today. But somewhere along the way, Israel forgot the melody and lost the words. Instead of listening to songs of remembrance and praise, they began to listen to the voice of their evil king. Unfortunately, it wasn't the first time. Many times in its history Israel had the same memory loss problem. Time and time again God proved He was the Great I AM, the GOD of Israel, yet they always seemed to forget His faithfulness. (For one example see Exodus 14:12.)

So Elijah rallied the people to come to Mount Carmel, and they were given front row seats to the best show in town. The problem was, they couldn't figure out for whom they were cheering.

- Fill in the blanks from verse 21 (NIV): "And Elijah came to all the people, and said, 'How long will you falter between _____ _____? If the _____ is God, follow Him; but if _____ is God, follow him.' But the people _____ _____.'"

The English Standard Version says it like this: "How long will you go *limping* between two different opinions?" (emphasis mine). God is the same whether or not we choose to believe Him. He is not changed by our circumstances. Unfortunately, we can be tempted to follow the squeakiest wheel at times. We can be swayed by the loudest, most persuasive voices, whether or not they speak the truth.

- What *voices* are you tempted to follow instead of listening to God's truth?
  - ____ the crowd/people pleasing
  - ____ the media/politics
  - ____ the media/Hollywood
  - ____ your family
  - ____ other: _____

There are a lot of opinions out there. And I know firsthand that it is hard to ignore these *voices*. Unfortunately I fall prey to the voice of the crowd sometimes. I am a people-pleaser by nature. But *people*—even well-meaning people—are not our god. Only God's opinion matters and it is His voice we should continue to seek in the midst of life's chaos.

- **Let's hear the Word of the Lord for us in these verses:**
  "If the Lord is God, follow Him; but if _____(insert your other
  voices **from above) is God, then follow (them)."**

It's time to choose who we are and who we are not going to listen to!

3. <u>Not listening (verses 25-29)</u>

This is one of those passages of Scripture that makes me laugh. God definitely has a sense of humor and He bestowed it upon Elijah. I remember when my husband preached a sermon about this passage of scripture. He said you can just hear Elijah's sarcasm when he says to the prophets of Baal, "Cry aloud, for he is a god; either he is meditating, or he is busy, or he is on a journey, or perhaps he is sleeping and must be awakened." My husband would know about sarcasm. He has a dry sense of humor, which is funny . . . most of the time. Unless he is teasing me! One Christmas I gave him a shirt to wear whenever he is in a sarcastic mood that said: "NATIONAL SARCASM SOCIETY: *like we need your support!*" Elijah could have joined the National Sarcasm Society too. That brother had some attitude!

The problem with the list of voices we are tempted to follow is that they seem to care about us . . . until we need them! We find them busy, distracted, or not listening. The credit card companies that say they care about our needs and want us to have it all seem to care . . . until we can't meet our minimum payment anymore. The other person that is not your spouse seems to care . . . until you get caught. The job that asks you to compromise your morals and integrity seems to care . . . the substances you turn to seem to care . . . the world you try so hard to impress with status and appearance seems to care. But these *idols* don't raise a finger for us when we need them. We willingly sacrifice our dignity, morals, health, family, and finances. But we are left hanging. The enemy taunts us: "Shout louder! Try harder!"

- Once again, the English Standard Version says in verse 26: "But there was no voice, and no one answered. And they *limped* around the altar that *they* had made" (emphasis mine). Has this ever happened to you? Did you rely too much on someone or something and ended up *limping*—left feeing lonely, burned, or used?

_____

_____

Well, we don't have to take it. We are on the winning team. Why do we listen to the wrong coach sometimes? The enemy may kick us and bruise us, but he cannot defeat us! *In Jesus's name we have the last word!*

- Whom did Elijah call on in verses 24 and 36?

_____

When my son, John David, was four years old, he was watching television and a scary commercial came on before we could change the channel. I saw an opportunity for a teaching moment and I expected to simply remind him that what we saw on television was not real and there was no reason to be scared. So I asked him, "Now what do we say about something scary that we see on television?" I burst out laughing when he replied, "GO AWAY IN JESUS'S NAME!"

In the name of Jesus we have all authority to tell the enemy to go away and that we will not listen to his lies anymore! When we call on the name of the Lord . . . something happens. There is power in the name of the Lord! Expect the Mighty Warrior Jesus to show up on the scene. The enemy does not stand a chance. In fact, he cannot stand at all in the presence of the supernatural name of Jesus (Phil. 2:9-11)!

The showdown! (verses 30-39)

It's time to get some attitude like Elijah, don't you think? I get tired of the enemy taunting me. I say it is time for us to turn the tables and show the enemy some attitude of our own! It is time to tell worry, temptation, and fear that we are not listening anymore! God is ready, willing, and able to come to our aid and show His glory when we call on His name.

- What did Elijah command the people to do in verses 33-34?

  _____

  _____

- After Elijah prayed, what happened to the sacrifice (v. 38)?

  _____

  _____

- **What was the people's response when they saw this (v. 39)?**

  _____

  _____

The Lord is God! He has proven Himself as faithful and true time and again. It is time for a showdown! And unlike the idols of this world, our God does not turn a deaf ear to our cries. Our God is listening. He is alive!! He is ready to do amazing things in our lives if we will listen for *His* voice beckoning us up our mountains to a place of victory.

POINT TO JESUS

WARMING UP

- Begin today by asking the Holy Spirit to speak to you through His Word.
- Please read 1 Kings 18:37-39.

ACT 2, SCENE 5

In a contest on a local radio station for Father's Day, the question was asked, "In one word, how would you describe your father?" I didn't enter the contest, but it got me thinking about how I would describe my dad. In one word I would have to say that he has been my *beacon*—a lighthouse pointing me in the right direction away from harm and always toward Jesus. As my earthly father, he has been very careful to help me see the greatness of my Heavenly Father and has modeled for me how to live a life that reflects Jesus.

My Dad was true to form not long ago when I shared with him something that was really troubling me. After listening, he empathized with me, knowing that I was hurting. But then he made a profound statement that changed my whole approach to the issue I was facing. He said, "You know, Susan Michelle, the enemy knows he will win if he can get you to focus on your problem and take your eyes off Jesus."

CRITERIA #1 for discerning God's voice: WHEN GOD SPEAKS, HE WILL POINT US TO JESUS.

There is no way to describe our Heavenly Father in just one word, but we can say that He is also our beacon. Like a proud Father, God could not wait to introduce us to His Son and sent a host of angels to shout his coming. God spared no drama as He sent out this extravagant birth announcement to the world (Luke 2:8).

- What else made God publicly shout from heaven?
  Matt. 3:16-17:

  _____

  Mark 9:2-7:

  _____

Our Heavenly Father points us to Jesus because:

- **Jesus is Lord!** In Revelation 19:16, what is Jesus called?

  _____

Read Ephesians 1:21. Where has Christ been placed by His Father?

_____

_____

- **Jesus is the only way to salvation.**
  What does John 14:6 say?

  _____

  _____

  According to Romans 6:23, from where does eternal life come?

  _____

  _____

- **God the Father revealed Himself through His Son.**
  Write John 14:10 here:

  _____

Our Heavenly Father knows that Jesus is all we need. And we point others to Jesus because we also know He is all they need!

In our Scripture passage today, Elijah had a tall order to help the Israelites get back on track. They had allowed their gaze to wander away from the one true God and now they were in a state of apathy and disillusionment. All they were focused on was their own need for rain. Ahab and Jezebel had led them astray in a perverted game of follow-the-leader.

- What was Elijah's prayer for the Israelites in verse 37?

  _____

  _____

God used Elijah to prophesy His *judgment* to a wicked and idolatrous nation and to point them back to the Lord. Then, God used John the Baptist as a first-century Elijah to prophesy His *grace* and point the nation to Jesus.

- How did Gabriel describe John the Baptist to his father, Zechariah, in Luke 1:17?

  _____

  _____

- In Malachi 4:5, what was Malachi's prophecy?

- **Jesus further explains to the crowds about John in Matthew 11:14. What did he say?**

  _____

  _____

Apparently Elijah and John the Baptist had more in common than the filling and power of the Holy Spirit. 2 Kings 1:8 describes Elijah as one who wore a garment of hair with a belt of leather around his waist. Matthew 3:4 states, "Now John wore a garment of camel's hair and a leather belt around his waist." Unfortunately, they also shared the same taste in fashion . . . or lack thereof!

But Elijah and John the Baptist did have something else in common: Their God-given mission to point others toward the coming of the Lord. And that, my friend, is definitely something worth sharing!

- According to John 1:23, what was John the Baptist's mission statement?

  _____

  _____

- What does it mean to "make straight the way of the Lord"?

  _____

  _____

Practically speaking, we make straight the way of the Lord by making Jesus as accessible as possible to the people around us. We must remove every barrier that may make it difficult for others to hear the message of Jesus Christ. And it starts with us.

1. We need to be different: Well, maybe not in our peculiar fashion statements like Elijah and John the Baptist. Cashmere, yes! Camel hair, no! But we should look different in our speech, attitudes, and the way we spend our time and resources. We should be authentic—full of integrity, maturity, and character.

- **What can you do to be different in your surroundings?**

  _____

  _____

2. We need to be aware of those around us: God is at work in the lives of those we live with, work with, and live near. If we are tuned in, God will make us aware of His activity in their lives.

- Pray for eyes to see, ears to hear, and wisdom to know how God wants to use you to reach out. Is He bringing anyone to your mind whom you can encourage in the faith?

  _____

  _____

3. We need to get to work: As Henry T. Blackaby states in his well-known Bible study, *Experiencing God*, "God's revelation is your invitation to join Him."[10] When the Holy Spirit has primed a heart to accept Him, it is our chance to make an eternal difference in the lives of others by pointing them to Jesus!

- Practically speaking, how can you *get to work* right now and make Jesus as accessible as possible to those the Lord has brought to your mind?

  _____

  _____

We have a vital role to play to be a beacon of light in a dark world. We too can come in the "spirit and power of Elijah," which is the Holy Spirit of God in us. We can proclaim the good news with power, tenacity, and courage as we prepare the way for the Lord to work in the lives of those around us. We know that Jesus is all this world needs. I love how little children raise their hand in Sunday school even before they know the question and always blurt out "Jesus" as their answer. We also know the answer to all of life's questions is Jesus. And we can point the way!

When my grandpa was a little boy, he had a puppy that followed him everywhere. One day before he went out to play, his mother told him to stay away from the pear tree because the pears were not ripe yet. But the temptation was just too much for him, so he checked to see if his mom was looking, climbed up into the tree, and enjoyed a not-so-ripe pear. He thought he had gotten away with his mischief until he came in for supper where his mom was unhappily waiting for him. When he asked her how she knew he had eaten the pear, she replied, "I looked out the window and did not see you. But I saw the dog sitting at the base of the pear tree, looking up and wagging his tail."

Let's point others to our Best Friend!

ACT 3

THE ROLE OF PRAYER

SCENE 1: SACRIFICE OF PRAISE

SCENE 2: A TIME FOR PRAYER

SCENE 3: THE HEART OF GOD

SCENE 4: PERSEVERING PRAYER

SCENE 5: THE HAND OF GOD

SACRIFICE OF PRAISE

WARMING UP

- Begin today by asking the Holy Spirit to speak to you through His Word.
- Please read 1 Kings 18:30-39.

ACT 3, SCENE 1

Drama, drama, drama. Duels with false prophets, miracles, bold confrontation of God's people gone rogue, defying Ahab and Jezebel, fire from heaven. Elijah's life certainly did not lack excitement. We may not go toe-to-toe with prophets of Baal, but our lives are filled with plenty of drama also, aren't they? Even though our lives are busy—especially because our lives are busy—making prayer a priority each day will keep us victorious over whatever life may bring that day.

This week we will begin the PREP STEP of PRAYER, and pick back up where we left off with Elijah on Mount Carmel. When we last saw him, Elijah had just defeated the prophets of Baal and had rallied the Israelites to worship God alone. Today we will begin our prayer week with Elijah's prayer for God to accept his sacrifice: And accept it He did!

So, let's ask ourselves: *Why did God so readily accept Elijah's prayer and how can we live lives equally as pleasing to God?*

THE FIRST REASON GOD ACCEPTED ELIJAH'S PRAYER:

    1.   Elijah offered a SACRIFICE OF PRAISE:

- How did Jesus teach us to begin our prayers in Luke 11:2?

  _____

- How do we enter God's presence according to Psalm 100:4?

  _____

According to Old Testament standards given by the Lord, Elijah was required to sacrifice to the Lord by very specific instructions. Leviticus 1-7 records these requirements from the Lord for burnt offerings, grain offerings, sin offerings, guilt offerings, and fellowship offerings that were to be given at specific times for specific purposes. But going through the motions was not what pleased God.

- Please read Psalm 51:16-17. What is God's view of empty sacrifices?

  _____

  _____

- **Now turn back to 1 Kings 18 and read verse 38 again. In reference to the verse in Psalm 51 above, why do you think God accepted Elijah's sacrifice?**

  _____

  _____

The whole point of offering a sacrifice out of worship, reverence, and repentance had become nothing better than just ritual for most of the Israelites in Elijah's day. They were *worshipping* all right, but they were worshipping all wrong!! They were so lukewarm they couldn't boil water if they were given fire from heaven . . .

- Write Hebrews 13:15 here:

  _____

  _____

  _____

We can offer our lives as living sacrifices to God. Jesus became the sacrificial Lamb for our sins.; therefore, burnt sacrifices are no longer needed. Because of Jesus, all God requires of us now is *our praise* from a heart of brokenness and worship! Obviously this is what God saw in Elijah's offering because He consumed Elijah's sacrifice quickly and completely. *God saw Elijah's heart.*

So, what is a *sacrifice of praise*? According to *Strong's Concordance*, the Hebrew translation of the word "sacrifice" is *minchah*, meaning "offering, gift, or present."[11] So by this definition we offer the Lord our "gift" of praise whenever we *choose* to praise Him, no matter what our circumstances may be. This can definitely feel like a sacrifice sometimes! Our very lives become an act of worship to the Lord when we make a sacrifice of praise during the good, the bad, and even during the funny!

- **In what practical ways can you offer God a sacrifice of praise during regular, everyday life?**

  _____

  _____

- How can you offer God a sacrifice of praise when you view life with humor? Is there something absurd that has happened to you that you can choose to laugh at and even learn from your mistake?

  _____

  _____

- Do you praise God in the midst of your pain? Let's worship together, right now, sweet friend. If you do nothing else today except stop here and pray, then I say we've had church! God cares for you and He knows your pain. He is more than able to bring you comfort and healing. But even before one prayer is answered, the Lord deserves your praise. Right now, bow your head and lay down your heartache at the foot of God's throne. Then praise Him anyhow. It will be accepted as a sweet aroma of praise! Read Psalm 42:5 and personalize it as your prayer below:

  _____

  _____

  _____

THE SECOND REASON GOD ACCEPTED ELIJAH'S PRAYER

    2.   Elijah's motivation was to GIVE GOD THE GLORY:

    a) ELIJAH'S PRAYER (verses 36-37)

- What was Elijah's motivation for offering this sacrifice?

_____

_____

    b) THE PEOPLE'S RESPONSE (verse 39)

- **What was the Israelite's response when God sent fire from heaven?**

_____

_____

Elijah did not ask God to answer so that everyone would say, "WOW! Look at Elijah! He is so powerful and amazing!" No, his prayer was that all would see God at work in his life and would say, "The LORD, He is God!"

    c) OUR RESPONSE

- According to Ephesians 1:12, what are we to be?

_____

_____

We are the praise of His glory. We are the applause of Christ. We are the magnifying glass through which God is made visible to the world. In other words, we were created to cause all eyes to turn to Jesus and bring Him glory. If we want the credit, we can be assured that we will only do what is in our own strength. And, I'm sorry, but that is not very amazing! We will not make a difference. But when the Lord goes with us for HIS glory, we will be amazed at all God will do! Each of us has been given special gifts and abilities that are to be used for God's glory. *But if others only see us and applaud our efforts and successes, we take away their chance to encounter the LORD.*

The motivation of our requests and petitions to the Father should ultimately be for His will and His glory. When God sees that we have a desire to show His glory to the world, He will show up in a display of His presence and power like we have never known! In verse 24, Elijah said, "The god who answers by fire—He is God!" Isaiah 4:4 reveals that God *is* the "Spirit of fire."

    d) GOD'S RESPONSE (verse 38)

- What was God's response in verse 38?

_____

_____

CRITERIA #2 for discerning God's voice: WHEN GOD SPEAKS IT WILL BE FOR HIS GLORY.

There will be no doubt that it is God when He answers your prayers. When God speaks, everything changes! Fear turns to courage, doubt turns to hope, and the messes we find ourselves in turn into miracles! Most importantly, it will point right back to Almighty God as the one and only who can do the impossible in our lives!

When we pray for God's glory, He does not just answer with a flicker of hope—He shows up with all-consuming power that dispels any doubt that He is the one true God. And He dispels any doubt that we may have about whether He has heard our prayers.

Ask Him to ignite a fire in your heart and HE WILL SHOW UP! Ask Him to bless your ministry to bring Him glory and HE WILL SHOW UP! Ask Him to perform a miracle in your family and marriage and HE WILL SHOW UP! Ask Him to be glorified through your circumstances and HE WILL SHOW UP!

- How do you need God to show up in your life right now?

_____

_____

Offer the Lord a sacrifice of praise and give Him all the glory in your life; He will be pleased with that type of prayer. Then all who see what God has done in you and for you and through you will say, "The LORD—He is God! The LORD—He is God!"

A TIME FOR PRAYER

WARMING UP

- Begin today by asking the Holy Spirit to speak to you through His Word.
- Please read 1 Kings 18:1; 41-42.

ACT 3, SCENE 2

Wow! Last week we had a very inspiring and exciting week as we witnessed how Elijah's obedience and bravery set the stage for some very *special effects*. Yesterday we saw why God accepted Elijah's prayer and sacrifice on Mount Carmel. But Elijah is not done praying yet. Now it is time for the lights to dim, the thunderous sound effects to quiet, and the crowds to go home. Elijah still has a major role to play. But this time his leading role is more behind the scenes. Now is a time for intercessory prayer.

THE SET:

- Look back at verses 1-2. Why did God originally send Elijah back to Ahab?

  _____

  _____

- Had this happened yet?

  _____

  _____

- **Where was Elijah in verse 42? What was he doing?**

  _____

  _____

Once again we can learn from Elijah's life how to experience the presence of God. And once again we will see that *hearing God comes from the preparation of our own hearts*. When we develop a relationship with the Lord through prayer, we will hear Him speaking, feel Him moving, and see Him answering. When Elijah needed to experience God, he knew the place to be was on his knees.

PREP STEP #2: PRAYER

The Lord proved on Mount Carmel that He was God and that Baal was not! But now Elijah needed another miracle. After three years of drought and famine, Ahab no longer had a sense of humor and Jezebel was on another rampage. Elijah's neck was on the line—literally! If there was no precipitation soon, Elijah's name would be mud (or dust in this case) because Elijah had promised that God would bring rain. But they had yet to feel the cool drops of rain on their parched mouths or hear the sizzle of water hit the dry land.

- When have you prayed for something that seemed to be God's will but the answer was a long time coming?

_____

_____

Elijah knew he was given an important role in the well-being of Israel's history. He knew that he was the instrument through which God would answer the prayers of Israel for much needed rain. He knew as a prophet of God Almighty that he was to bring the Word of the Lord to the people and carry the burdens of the people back to God. And he knew that none of this would happen unless he spent time on his knees. He became not only prophet, but intercessor.

God is looking for those, like Elijah, who are willing to lift up prayers for a broken world. Because of Elijah's intercession a widow's life had been saved (1 Kings 17:16), she had seen her son raised from the dead (1 Kings 17:23), and Israel had witnessed the power of the LIVING God on Mount Carmel (1 Kings 18:38). Now Israel awaited much needed relief from drought.

A refusal to seek the Lord as their one true God had led Israel into slavery, captivity, bondage, disease, and suffering. Psalm 106:15 describes it as a *wasting disease*. Like Israel, there is a wasteland around us that needs much intercession for its healing.

- **What has become acceptable in our country that is clearly sin?**

_____

- **What symptoms do we see of a *wasting disease* in our country, our physical bodies, and our souls due to our rebellion?**

_____

It is imperative that we learn to recognize our symptoms of disobedience so that we can humbly fall before the Lord and receive healing and restoration. When we are dry spiritually we may seek other ways to quench our thirst, *but we were created to seek the Lord to be satisfied.* (See Jeremiah 2:13.) When we are cracked and dry we will see the consequences of sin in our lives, our families, our marriages, and our country. Disease caused by sexual immorality, corrupt politics, violence, the abuse of the innocent, and premature deaths of the unborn are just a few of many examples of our drought-stricken souls. Like Israel, we desperately need God to rain down His healing upon our land.

A) <u>Prayer for our country</u>:

I have to be honest. When things are going smoothly for our country I can forget to pray for our nation and our leaders. But when things look shaky, I crank it up a notch.

- What about you? On a scale of 1-10, how are you at praying for your country during *good times*? _____ What about times of crisis? _____

- Look up 2 Chronicles 7:14. What four things are we to do when we pray for our land?

  _____

  _____

- In what three ways will God respond when we seek Him in prayer this way?

  _____

  _____

- **According to 1 Timothy 2:1-4, what four things are we to do?**

  _____

- **For whom?**

  _____

- **What will be the result?**

  _____

These Scriptures do not say, "When the government leaders or sinners in your country will pray . . ." It is a command for "My people" to pray and then God will hear from heaven. Like Elijah, we have been given the awesome responsibility as God's children to hold up our land in prayer. The future of our land lies heavily in our hands and on our knees.

As King Solomon wrote in Ecclesiastes: "There is nothing new under the sun . . ." The problems of a corrupt, lost, wayward, spiritually declining nation were not isolated to ancient Israel. Most of our world can be characterized the same way in these last days. Depressing, huh?! But there is good news! Prayer still makes a difference. God still hears. God still cares. And God still moves!!

B) Prayer for ourselves:

God has a plan to bring light into the darkness . . . first *to* us and then *through* us! Do you ever wonder why you may not hear the Lord speak clearly in your life? Do you want to experience God in a fresh, powerful way? Then you have a role to play . . . behind the scenes . . . on your knees . . . for your own vibrant friendship with Jesus.

- We cannot cast blame for the problems we face as a country, in our homes, and even in our churches if our own failure to spend time with God in prayer causes us to dry up like a parched land. *When each one begins to take responsibility for personal revival, the world will naturally be changed.*
- Take a moment to pray for yourself and confess any attempt to fill your thirst and hunger with anything other than the presence of the Lord. Confess any lack of seeking Him with your whole heart through regular prayer and study of His word. Then ask God to begin a revival in your own heart.

When you have done this, you are ready for the important role God has for you to play as intercessor in this world!

God's great compassion and love for us adds a beautiful twist to the story of our lives. He has already written the script to include each of us as a key player in the story. Without our prayers, the ending does not include many of the people that were supposed to be *on the scene*. But when we fall to our knees and humbly ask for God's mercy and help in our time of need, He is anxious and ready to answer us!

THE HEART OF GOD

WARMING UP

- Begin today by asking the Holy Spirit to speak to you through His Word.
- Please read 1 Kings 18:1 and 41-42.

ACT 3, SCENE 3

Don't you love the smell of rain when it is coming? I believe Elijah could smell it, hear it and almost taste it. The coming of the rain was the coming of a long-awaited answer to prayer for Israel.

- Look back at 1 Kings 18:1. What did God ask Elijah to do?

_____

_____

Elijah always seemed to know exactly what to pray for and how to receive God's answers. How can we do the same? How do we know we are praying for God's will? How can we pray with confidence? For Elijah, and for us, one key to the effectiveness of our prayers is _knowing God's heart_.

- **According to Ephesians 6:17-18, how can we know God's heart?**

_____

_____

Prayer is what changes us from knowing _about_ God, to truly _knowing_ God. There is a great connection between praying for God's will to be done, as Jesus taught us to pray, and our prayers being answered. "Intercession originates from God's heart."[12]

Prayer is the backstage, behind-the-scenes work that is done one-on-one with the author of our lives that helps us know His heart and His plan. Through prayer we learn God's will, but often just one scene at a time. We don't get to read all the ACTS ahead of time. So it is much like living improv with God—taking our cues from Him each day as we spend time in prayer. Our Sovereign Lord is in control of all things. There is no doubt. But God has given His children a very special invitation to be a part of His work around us. God's will _will_ be done. The question is: Will we accept His invitation to be a part of it?

Do we dare pray for God's heart to be superimposed onto ours? Be forwarned: When we pray for His heart, we need to be ready to feel pain and hurt and unexplainable compassion. Anne Graham Lotz says, "I want to have a strong heart, but I don't want to be hard-hearted, so I have asked the Lord to break my heart with the things that break His. And the only way I can know the things that break His heart is to ask Him in prayer, then listen as He tells me through His

Word. That's how I know those things that have made me cry out to Him have made Him cry first."[13]

I had an "aha moment" that transformed my prayer journey. I felt overwhelmed by so many needs—including myself, family, friends, church, our nation, and needs around the world. So I asked the Lord to give me His heart and to teach me how to pray. Very soon something interesting began to happen. I began to wake during the night almost physically sick with a desire to pray for abused children. This seemed a little random to me since I had no background of abuse. But my thoughts and heart began to pour out in anguish for these children I had never met. That is when I realized God had answered my prayer to teach me how to pray more effectively: *He had given me His heart!* There was no doubt what I was to pray for . . . my heart was so heavy that I *had* to pray.

- According to Romans 8:26, how do we know what to pray?

  _____

- Who teaches us how to pray?

  _____

- How is He helping us?

  _____

The people God has placed in our lives (e.g., family, friends, church) are those we have been given a responsibility to regularly hold up in prayer. But beyond this important role, sometimes we are also given a deep desire to pray for a special issue or person that desperately needs God's touch at that time. *God's compassion becomes our passion!* Hear this beautiful quote from Richard J. Foster's classic, *Celebration of Discipline:* "If we have God-given compassion and concern for others, our faith will grow and strengthen as we pray. In fact, if we genuinely love people, we desire for them far more than it is within our power to give, and that will cause us to pray."[14]

- What person(s) or situation(s) makes your heart so heavy that you *have* to pray?

  _____

- **James 5:17-18 says, "Elijah was a man _____ _____ _____; he prayed earnestly that it would not rain, and it did not rain on the land for three and a half years. Again he prayed, and the heavens gave rain, and the earth produced its crops" (NIV).**
- **Now write vv. 13-16 here:**

  _____

  _____

  _____

Elijah was not a fictional character in a play. He was a real man, just like us. The close relationship he had with God in prayer is just as attainable for us. I believe that the prayers of the righteous are effective. I do. But I sometimes feel that my prayers are more frustrated than fervent. It is a spiritual discipline that I constantly have to work at and I can suffer from guilt when I fear I have not prayed enough, forgot to pray for someone I had promised to remember, or am unsure of unanswered prayers.

- How about you? Do you ever suffer from *prayer anemia* (not enough prayer)?
  Yes _____ No _____
- or *prayer paranoia* (worry about not praying enough)?
  Yes _____ No _____
- or *prayer disorientation* (confusion about how to pray)?
  Yes _____ No _____

Prayer is not supposed to feel unattainable—just intentional. It is not an impossible discipline—just purposeful. It is hard to imagine that Elijah was "a man just like us." Richard J. Foster says, "Many of us are discouraged rather than challenged by . . . those 'giants of faith.' But rather than flagellating ourselves for our obvious lack, we should remember that God always meets us where we are and slowly moves us along into deeper things."[15]

- **How can unbelief about the effectiveness of our prayers cause us to miss out instead of witness miracles?**

  _____

It is easy to sell ourselves and our prayers short, but what we believe about our prayers ultimately reflects what we believe about our God. I don't want to miss out on anything God has in store for me or those I love that could be unlocked through prayer. I want to believe that my prayers are moving mountains.

What a disappointment when we eat crumbs from the floor when God's banquet table is before us. What would our walk with Christ be like if we spent our time seeking Him with all our heart, soul, mind, and strength? What would our church be like if we chose to believe that our prayers truly mattered and knew revival was ours for the asking? What would our neighborhood, our family, and our friends experience if we truly believed that our prayers were making a difference?

- What would you like to ask God to do? Ask Him in the form of a written prayer below to give you a faith-shot in the arm as you pray:

  _____

  _____

I don't want to miss out on the relationship of knowing God as He reveals His heart to me in prayer. I want to experience God's still, small voice and allow Him to change my ordinary days into extraordinary moments with Him, don't you? Elijah was a man just like us, and he believed he could make a difference. Ask God to give you His heart and then pray with confidence that you are moving the hand of God.

The answer to Israel's prayers, and ours, are just on the horizon!

PERSEVERANT PRAYER

WARMING UP

- Begin today by asking the Holy Spirit to speak to you through His Word.
- Please read 1 Kings 18:42 and Phil. 1:6.

ACT 3, SCENE 4

In yesterday's study we recognized that God had not yet answered Elijah's prayer for rain. Elijah knew God's plan was to send the rain, and Elijah believed God would be faithful. But that did not ensure an easy or quick answer to his prayers. The issue still required much prayer and Elijah was called to persevere.

- In verse 42, what did Elijah do?

_____

In other words: HE FELL FLAT ON HIS FACE! Being on our face before the Lord is an appropriate response to His holiness. It is always the place to begin. Of course, we can pray in any posture, any place, anytime. But the literal act of bowing before the Lord as we begin to pray does several things. It reminds us:

1. That God is the Holy King and that He deserves to be honored: Bowing before the Lord is not only a deserving response to God's holiness, but when we truly encounter the Lord in a place of worship in our hearts, there is no other response we are capable of—except to fall flat on our face in awe, reverence, and fear of the Lord. That is where Elijah started.

2. Of the surrender of our lives to God and for His will to be done in us: When we begin our prayers with this type of humble attitude, God is pleased. (See Psalms. 51:16-17.)

3. Of our need . . . that we can't possibly make it without the help of the Lord.

When I am really distraught, I crumble in a heap before the Lord, don't you? It is a posture that says, "Without you, Lord, I can't make it one more step!" It is earnest, perseverant, stubborn prayer. And, most often, it is desperate prayer!

Parenting has brought many, many opportunities for me to fall flat on my face in prayer. Looking back I have to laugh at being first-time parents and how overwhelmed we often found ourselves. We were new parents, and we did all the new parent things: We read books on parenting; went to childbirth classes; read each manual for the crib, car seat, and high chair . . . and we sang to the baby in the womb. It wasn't because we were hoping he would be born a child prodigy—knowing children's classics like "Jesus Loves Me" and "Twinkle, Twinkle, Little Star." *We just wanted him to know us and to know our voice.* The only problem was that we did not know Matthew was breach. So all that time that we thought we were singing right into his ears . . . it was actually the other end! Poor kid had not even been born yet and his parents were already embarrassing him!

But there was one song in particular that God wanted *us* to know as parents. It was not a children's classic, but it became the theme song of our parenting lives. Here is the story of how we stumbled across this song and how we discovered that it was actually God speaking . . .

The day I went in for my pregnancy test, I was working as a physician assistant. I ran over to the lab on my break, took the test with great anticipation, and then went back to work. Of course my mind was elsewhere and I probably prescribed hair plugs for women and hormone therapy for men. But thankfully I had no complaints! Then, after an excruciating wait, a Christian friend of mine, Michelle, showed up from the lab with the results. But she didn't say anything; instead she just began to sing words from Philippians 1:6: "He who began a good work in you will be faithful to complete it in you."

I had my answer! It was not only an answer to my pregnancy test, but would forever be a promise. God had begun something new in me and He was in control! Two days later, while visiting one of our favorite churches on a Valentine Sunday, my husband and I could not believe what happened next. The screens on each side of the sanctuary flashed the Scripture of the day: "Being confident of this, that he who began a good work in you will carry it on until the day of Christ Jesus" (Phil. 1:6 NIV). Just like the song Michelle sang to me! We looked down at the bulletin and there again was the Scripture printed before us. And, as if that were not enough, the preacher then stood and proclaimed to the congregation in a loud voice, "He who began a good work in you will carry it on until the day of Christ Jesus!"

Now, I know I am not quick, but I got the message. I guess God wanted to make sure I didn't miss it!

- Write Philippians 1:6 here, but this time insert your name and/or the names of those you love instead of the word "you":

_____

_____

_____

Little did we know how soon we would need that promise. Since then we have been blessed with two wonderful boys, but it has not always been an easy ride. To spare the details, let's just say the boys have had more than their share of physical difficulties. Yet through all the sleepless nights, specialists, doctor visits, hospital stays, and medical bills, we held onto our promise: *A promise that God is in control and He is not finished with us yet.*

You have been given the same promise. "He who began a good work in you will perfect it until the day of Christ Jesus." God wants you to get the message! And whether you hear it through a song, a scripture, a preacher, or this study . . . it is still your promise too! Do you have a difficult situation in your life that just does not seem to budge even though you pray and pray? Do you sometimes feel discouraged about your health, job, finances, home life, or spiritual life? Do you feel unfinished, incomplete, and not amused? Don't give up because God has not given up on you! Chances are, He may be using some of those circumstances to mature you, teach you, and to help complete the work He has started in you or those you love.

- Is anything discouraging you about your personal or spiritual life right now? If so, what is it?

  _____

  _____

- **Please turn to Romans 5:3-5 (NIV) and fill in the blanks below:**
  "because we know that _____ produces _____;
  perseverance, _____; and character, _____."
- **According to this Scripture, how do you think our sufferings turn into hope?**

  _____

  _____

This Scripture has been especially dear to me when I struggle with perseverance while faced with unanswered prayer or suffering. No one chooses to suffer and we certainly do not want to see those we love go through hard times. Unfortunately, suffering is no respecter of persons. But from then on it is our choice what we do with our circumstances. Only when we trust God with our circumstances are we given the strength to persevere. Only when we quit kicking our feet and pounding our fists like a child who thinks they deserve an easy life do we gain character. And only when we allow the Father to become all we need . . . do we find hope! *Hope is found in the Lord when He becomes the focus and not our circumstances.* When everything else in life is up for grabs, grab onto Him and your hope will stand firm.

I can't wait to share with you one more thing about the connection between waiting on the Lord in prayer and our hope. The original Hebrew word for hope is *Yachal,* which means: 1) to wait, to hope, to expect.[16] *In other words, our hope actually comes from the wait . . . not the answer!* When we wait, pray, persevere, and tarry, we are actively living out our faith in the Lord. And this hope in the Lord causes an expectation to birth in us that God has something good in store for those who wait upon Him. For those who don't give up. For those who believe!

- **Read Zephaniah 3:17. What is God doing?**

  _____

  _____

Precious child of God, stay on your face in prayer. He is not finished yet. And as you wait, listen for the voice of your Father as He sings over you. Because He wants you to know His voice.

THE HAND OF GOD

WARMING UP

- Begin today by asking the Holy Spirit to speak to you through His Word.
- Please read 1 Kings 18:43-46.

ACT 3, SCENE 5

Finally, after three and a half years of waiting, Israel was about to receive her answer to prayer. Today we will join Elijah on his knees and follow Elijah's example of trusting God's heart until we can see His hand.

1. ### Expect a miracle (v. 43):

   - **What did Elijah have his servant do, according to verse 43?**

     _____

     _____

   - What did the servant report back to Elijah in verse 43?

     _____

     _____

   - **How many times did Elijah send him back?**

     _____

     _____

Elijah *expected* a miracle. Truly believing that God is listening and that He will give us what we ask for is another key to receiving the answer to our prayers. Our faith brings expectation. And expectation proves our faith.

   - Please read Luke 18:1-5. Summarize these verses in your own words.

     _____

     _____

     _____

Verse 5 says that the judge answered the widow's request so that she would not "eventually wear him out with her coming." Then, in verse 7, "And will not God bring about justice for His chosen ones, who cry out to him day and night?" Children are especially good at persevering (aka whining). My kids can be so creative in the way they keep rephrasing their requests. They know that if I think it is in their best interest I often will give in, in one way or another. They can truly "wear me out in their coming!"

We are actually told to approach prayer in this manner (well, maybe minus the whining). We must trust that God sees the big picture and will do what is best. But we must also expect Him to answer. Jesus said, "Therefore I tell you, whatever you ask for in prayer, *believe* that you have received it, and it will be yours" (Mark 11:24, emphasis mine).

- Write a prayer to God that you believe He will answer your requests, even if you have been praying for a long time.

_____

_____

2. __As small as a man's hand (v. 44):__

I can't tell you how excited I am at this moment. All the waiting and praying and expecting has come to this moment when God answers Elijah's prayers. I am excited because I know this Scripture is not just for us to read as a story, but to apply to our own lives. We can expect Him to come through for us too!

- **What did the servant report back to Elijah in verse 44a?**

_____

_____

The breezes that come before a storm were beginning to blow. So Elijah said, "Go and tell Ahab, 'Hitch up your chariot and go down before the rain stops you.'" *Elijah recognized God's answer and began to act in faith.*

All we need is a glimpse of God's hand to know He is at work in our lives, bringing about His answer to our prayers. Even if we cannot see the big picture yet, we can see evidence of God's work all around us. "Learning to recognize God's answer to our prayers is critical because answered prayer is one of the powerful ways God speaks to us."[17] When we see answers to our prayers we are, in essence, hearing God say to us, "Yes. I heard you. I am here. And now it is time for you see that I have been working on your behalf all along to answer your prayers."

I once heard Nazarene missionary, Fred Huff, preach about an experience so similar to Elijah's prayer for rain that I knew it should be a part of this day of our study together. With his blessing, let me tell you the story:

> On a horseback riding evangelism trip to Lesotho, Africa, Fred and his companions were given permission to have an outdoor service for villagers who had never heard the gospel message before. High in the mountains these people sat down wearing colorful clothing, tepee-shaped hats, and corncob pipes. As they listened and sang, the villagers also kept murmuring something in their local dialect. When asked what they were saying, Fred was told they said, "Let the rains come." The interpreter said, "We've had drought in the area and desperately need rain. They are saying if you know God as you say you do, and if He is as powerful as you say He is, then let Him bring rain and they will believe." As the service progressed, Fred Huff continued to look down the mountain for a "cloud the size of a man's hand." Then he saw it. At first it was small, but as it moved up the mountain it got larger and larger. Then just as the Bible was opened to preach . . . the rains came. Not just a drizzle, but a deluge. A downpour! There were even hailstones mixed in as if

God were saying to the people, "You want to see a little of My power?" After the rain stopped, Fred preached a simple gospel message and twenty-one adults stepped forward to accept the Lord Jesus Christ as their Savior!

God is faithful and able to answer when we call on Him! Like Fred Huff's prayer for rain in a desperate, ominous time, we also come before the Lord at times with serious requests, and God is faithful to meet those needs. But we can also recognize God's presence and voice as He actively meets our everyday, ordinary needs. It just occurred to me as I was writing this chapter that God had answered a request for me that did not seem like something serious enough to agonize in prayer about—yet it was important to me. I was leaving for a trip and could not find a kennel to keep my dog because it was a holiday weekend. I fretted over it and asked God to help us figure out what to do. But then I forgot to ask anyone else to help. Two days before we left I decided we must take the dog on a two-day trip with us since I had not made any other arrangements. Then, without being asked, a lady from our church called and asked if she could keep our dog for us while we were gone. I tried to tell her what an answer to prayer she was, but I still don't think she understood how much her obedience to God's promptings spoke to me. Not only was she so in tune with His Spirit that she heard Him asking her to call us, but I was blown away that God had heard my tiny prayer for my dog.

I felt God say to me, "I am listening and I am working on your behalf." What a great God we serve. He not only brings rain to a parched land when the people need to see His active presence in their lives, but He also brings answers to our most unimpressive prayers! God is good, all the time!

- Where do you see the evidence of the Lord working in or around you?

  _____

  _____

3. <u>**The power of the Lord (vv. 45-46):**</u>

- Write verse 45 in the space below.

  _____

  _____

  _____

We can be assured that God has heard our prayers and is acting on our behalf. A storm is coming with more of God's goodness than we can think or imagine. We can begin to act in faith—thanking and praising Him for His answers. *Then, when we see God's hand at work, it is time to get off our knees and get busy!*

That is exactly what Elijah did. But he always has to do things in such dramatic fashion, doesn't he?

Read verse 46 and fill in the blanks below (NIV).

- "The _____ ____ _____ _____ came upon Elijah and tucking his _____ into his belt, he _____ _____ of Ahab ____ _____ _____ to Jezreel."

Obviously to beat the storm, Ahab would have had his horses running at full speed. Poor Elijah had to run in a dress (aka his "cloak"), but that didn't stop him. Through the power of the Lord, Elijah ran faster than a chariot of horses and beat Ahab to Jezreel. That is approximately six miles! No special effects or stunt-doubles needed in this episode. No horsepower needed, either. Elijah had the power of the Lord!

That is the result of prayer! There is power in prayer, not only to bring about answers, but to fill us with the Holy Spirit's presence. We may not run as fast as horses, like Elijah, but the power of the Holy Spirit in our lives gives us the ability to do what we otherwise cannot do on our own. And that is definitely a miracle!

- **When have you experienced the power of God in your life to do what you could not have done on your own?**

_____

That is why we pray: To admit that we are helpless on our own and in need of One greater than ourselves, One that is able to do "immeasurably more than we can think or imagine" (Ephesians 3:20). We pray to experience the provisions of God and the power of God. And we pray to experience the voice of God.

We witness God's power when we see Him at work around us. But we can also trust His heart when we have yet to see His hand. *Expect a miracle.* Act in faith and get ready for God to rain down His goodness. Keep looking to the sky, because He is ever faithful!

- Set aside a day this week to "pray without ceasing." Ask God to help make you aware of His presence as go throughout your day. Ask Him to direct your every step. Then journal here how you experienced the provisions or power or voice of God as you walked with Him in prayer throughout your day.

_____

_____

_____

_____

ACT 4

THE ROLE OF GOD'S WORD AND BEING STILL

SCENE 1: THE WORD OF GOD—PART 1

SCENE 2: THE WORD OF GOD—PART 2

SCENE 3: TOO MUCH FOR YOU

SCENE 4: BEING STILL

SCENE 5: SPEAKING OF LOVE

THE WORD OF GOD: PART 1

WARMING UP

- Begin today by asking the Holy Spirit to speak to you through His Word.
- Please read 1 Kings 17:2; 17:8; 18:1; 19:9; 19:11; 19:13; 19:15; 21:17; 21:28; and 2 Kings 1:3; 1:15.

ACT 4, SCENE 1

When I first began writing this Bible study, I asked several people, "If you could hear God speak in an audible voice, what would you ask Him?" Their responses ranged anywhere between "Why did Jesus have to die the way he did?" to "Uhhhh . . ."

- **What would you ask God if you could hear Him answer you in an audible voice?**

_____

This week you and I will follow Elijah up Mount Sinai in his quest—and ours—to seek the Lord. Our theme for this week is twofold: The Word of God and Being Still. These are the last two PREP STEPS in our study as we continue our journey to hear the Gentle Whispers of God. These PREP STEPS are linked together this week because God's Word is, obviously, God's words to us. But we must *be still* and meditate on His Word in order for it to apply to our lives. They must go together or we are in danger of the Bible being merely information for our minds. We want it to transform our lives!

- Look at the Warming Up Scriptures above. In each reference, how did the Lord speak to Elijah?

_____

Elijah received a clear message from the Lord. The Word of the Lord came to Him. That's all we know. We are not sure in what form the Word of the Lord came each time—sometimes His voice was heard, sometimes an angel appeared, and sometimes we are not given the details. Hebrews 1:1 says, "In the past God spoke to our ancestors through the prophets at many times and in various ways" (NIV).

- **Let's discover a few of those "ways" God spoke:**
  Gen. 19:1-13 _____

  Deut. 18:18 _____

  Gen. 28:12 _____

Num. 34:13 _____

Num. 27:21 _____

1 Sam. 3:4 _____

Ex. 3:1-4 _____

Dan 5:5 _____

Num. 22:28 _____

Ex. 33:11 _____

We are not always told specifically how God spoke, "but the Bible is clear that when God spoke, the people knew it was God, they knew what he was going to do, and they knew what their response should be."[18] I don't know about you, but I am tempted to think, "No fair! I'm sure I would know what the Lord said to me if an angel showed up, or if I saw writing on the wall, or if my pet started talking to me!" But the most important thing is not the HOW, but the WHO. God still speaks—there is no doubt! He can still speak today in any way He chooses, but we have something more consistent, clear, and accessible than any prophet of old . . . we have the entire Word of God at our fingertips!

PREP STEP #3: THE WORD OF GOD

From creation to Revelation, we have the entire plan; the entire set; the completed series; the behind-the-scenes, backstage peek of God's plan, God's ways, and God's heart. God is faithful to speak to us and His words are right there for us, but we must get up and seek Him through His Word. It cannot be impressed upon our hearts and bound to our foreheads unless we immerse our selves in it. (See Deuteronomy 6:8.)

- How often are we to read the Bible according to Deuteronomy 17:19 and Psalms 119:97?

_____

- How would you say you are at reading the Bible as these Scriptures direct? Are you satisfied with your efforts or would you like to change in some way?

_____

I commend each of you for committing to this study. I am truly proud of you! His Word will not return void in your life, but will accomplish what He desires and will achieve the purpose for which He sent it. (See Isaiah 55:11.) Bible study is so important and vital to our spiritual ears, because when we immerse ourselves in God's Word daily it will:

1.   Apply to your circumstances.

When we study the Bible it intersects with our lives. God has given us a template for life. He has given us His Word and invites us to superimpose our circumstances onto this template. When you read His Word, your name, your life, and your circumstances begin to fill in the white spaces between the lines of Scripture.

While studying and writing this Bible study, God used these passages in 1 and 2 Kings to apply to my life so often right when and where I needed it. When I was burned out and distressed, He reminded me to *be still*. When I felt alone, He sent me an Elisha. When I felt distant, He reminded me of our PREP STEPS and helped me apply them to my own life. The truth is—I could have been studying the book of Malachi and it would have transformed my life. Praise God, His Word is alive and active (Heb. 4:12)!

- **When has the Bible come to life for you right when you needed it during this study or another time?**

  _____

  _____

  _____

- **What does 2 Timothy 3:16 say God's Word will do for us?**

  _____

  _____

Read back over those words. As we just learned, the Bible applies to our circumstances and is clearly used for teaching us His ways. But what about those other verbs: Rebuking, correcting, training? Those are not warm-fuzzy words. It is sometimes a tough pill to swallow, but we need to allow God to guide us and direct us even if it is hard to hear.

The first time I ever got up enough nerve to send in something I wrote to a magazine, I quickly received a manila envelope from them in the mail. (The hasty response should have been my first clue as to what was inside.) I was too nervous to open it, so I had my husband read it to me right there by the mailbox. The very first sentence started with the words, "Your manuscript has been rejected due to . . ." My heart sank and I held back the tears long enough to get alone inside. Then, I poured out my heart to God and asked why He would give me the desire to share His Word with others . . . just to get my heart stepped on. Yes . . . pitiful. Can you picture the pity-party? I knew my own mind would play tricks on me, so I went to my Bible for comfort and guidance. I don't usually use the *open-and-point* method when reading the Bible, but this day His words seemed to be highlighted for me as soon as I opened my Bible. It fell open to Ecclesiastes 5:2: "Do not be hasty with your mouth, do not be hasty in your heart to utter anything before God. God is in heaven and you are on earth, so let your words be few!" Not necessarily the words of comfort and cheer that I had hoped for! I wasn't in the mood for God's sense of humor, but this verse certainly put everything in perspective. I obeyed, and you know what happened? I stilled my heart and my mouth and just received what His Word had for me. Then I became more and more acutely aware of God's presence in my own life and had more to share later when the timing was right for God's plans instead of my own. It is worth it to listen when God speaks to us through His Word—even when it is hard to hear—because He knows what will bring us abundant life.

2. God's Word gives us life!

When we immerse ourselves in God's Word daily and apply it to our life, it changes us. Changing is hard work. Changing is not for wimps, but allowing God's Word to mold us brings great reward. It must break God's heart sometimes when we just take what life brings without allowing the Bible to help us make sense of it. Other than not accepting Christ as Savior, the saddest thing to our Lord must be watching us not live life to the fullest. He wants us to experience the joy that comes from letting Him transform our days from lifeless to life changing!

In our Scripture above from 2 Timothy 3:16, the word "inspired" is used in many translations, including the American Standard Version. "God-breathed" is used in the New International Version. In the English Standard Version it is written as "breathed out by God."

- **What are God's words to us according to John 6:63b (NIV):**

_____

_____

"In the beginning was the Word, and the Word was with God, and the Word was God" (John 1:1). His Word created life! What God breathed into Adam and into all of creation, He breaths into us through His "God-breathed" Word . . . LIFE. When we read the inspired Word of God, we hear God speak to us right where we are. We allow God to transform and change us. We let Him breathe life into our ordinary days. And, best of all, we experience Jesus, the Word of God made flesh.

THE WORD OF GOD: PART 2

WARMING UP

- Begin today by asking the Holy Spirit to speak to you through His Word.
- Please read 1 Kings 19:1-4.

ACT 4, SCENE 2

God's Word is alive and active. (See Hebrews 4:12.) When we immerse ourselves in Scripture, God will undoubtedly shower us with His guidance, encouragement, power, correction, and peace. These things are God's voice being written on the tablets of our hearts!

As you study a particular passage, God will speak to you through His Holy Spirit during your time of study, or He may use that Scripture later in your day or later in your week to shed light on a decision you must make, a tweak you might need to make in an action or your attitude, encouragement on hard days, or even to be reminded of His presence right when you need it.

But life is so busy! And there are so many things that threaten to distract us from hearing God's voice. Can we really trust that what we are hearing is from God? How can we be sure it is God? I am so glad you asked! The good—no, *great*—news is that we *can* hear Him in the midst of our busy lives and we *can* have discernment to know it is God. In fact, in the midst of everyday life is precisely when He speaks. Very rarely do we get to go to Mount Horeb to hear God whisper to us. But we definitely have our own "earthquakes, winds, and fires" to deal with that can distract us from His voice. Thank the Lord that He also knows how to get our attention in the mall, doing the dishes, and taking the dog for a walk. For me, it's usually somewhere between making a peanut butter and jelly sandwich and the dry cleaners.

Yet we can easily mistake other "voices" for the Lord's. We are bombarded by advice from friends and family (whether or not we asked for it), the influence of media, self-help books, new age movements that tell us to listen to ourselves and to be our own god, other Christian leaders, and even our own minds when we might want something so badly that we talk ourselves into believing that "God told us."

- **How do you think we can really know if it is God speaking or not?**

  _____

  _____

- **Read Acts 17:11. What did the Bereans do?**

  _____

  _____

Life deals us quite a few True/False tests and we are in need of the answer key. Psalm 119:105 calls God's Word "a lamp to my feet and a light to my path" (HCSB). Not only does God speak to us clearly through the Bible, but also He uses His Word as our answer key to confirm to us whether or not what we are *hearing* is from Him.

CRITERIA #3 for discerning God's voice: WHEN GOD SPEAKS IT WILL ALWAYS BE CONFIRMED THROUGH HIS WORD

We can test what we hear against Scripture. The Bible trumps our own opinions, others' advice, or Satan's lies. "The Bible is the standard by which everything else is measured."[19] The Lord will never speak anything to you that does not line up with the Bible. At times we may feel His gentle correction, but His purpose in Scripture is for us to become more like Him, to give us encouragement, gain wisdom, and find guidance for our circumstances (2 Timothy 3:16-17).

- Please read Psalm 145:8-9; 13. What do these verses say about God's nature?

_____

_____

_____

God is good—only good. He is loving and compassionate and gracious even when we do not understand His ways. And here is a truth that you can take to the bank: He loves you (John 3:16) and He can only speak to you in agreement with who He is—loving and good.

I have a close friend who shared with me her struggle with self-confidence every time she was around a more put-together person. Even though they were good friends, she could not help but compare herself to her friend whenever they were together. So I asked her, "Where in the Bible does it support those kinds of thoughts about you? If it is not God talking, then who is?" Anytime we weigh negative thoughts against God's Word, those thoughts will come up wanting. (See Philippians 4:8-9.)

- What about you? When has an *inner or external voice* not been the voice of truth for you?

_____

_____

If you were able to answer that question, then you are in good company. Elijah is known for many of his *mountaintop* moments with the Lord, but he also had some very *valley* moments in which he needed to sift out the truth from deceiving circumstances. The good news is that he applied God's truth to many of the situations he found himself in. The bad news is that sometimes he didn't apply God's truth to situations he found himself in.

It made all the difference in how he experienced life when he listened to the truth. When Elijah heeded God's words to him he was confident, he had God's power to perform miracles, he had a fiery attitude to take on anything or anybody, he had supernatural strength and energy, he led others to recognize truth, and he had acute hearing of God's gentle whispers. But when Elijah failed to apply God's truth to his own life, he became defeated, depressed, afraid, weak, lonely, and confused.

- **What was Jezebel's threat to Elijah in 1 Kings 19:1-2?**

  _____

  _____

- **What was Elijah's response in verses 3-4?**

  _____

  _____

- **What was the truth according to 1 Kings 18:37-39? Did Elijah need to fear Jezebel?**

  _____

  _____

Elijah had pointed the Israelites to the truth on Mount Carmel—that the LORD is God and none other. Now he needed to apply it to himself and seek truth in the midst of his own difficult circumstances. Truth is our weapon against the enemy. Satan loves to drive a wedge between us and the Lord by making us question if the Lord is God and whether He is "God enough" for all of our situations. Satan tried to make the Israelites question *"IF* God is really God . . ." (1 Kings 18:21, emphasis mine). And he tempted Jesus in the desert by saying, *"IF* you are the Son of God . . ." (Matthew 4:1-11, emphasis mine). How can we hear the *still, small voice* of God when the enemy is screaming in our ears?

- In summary, how did Jesus fight Satan's lies in Matthew 4:1-11?

  _____

"Satan is a master at deception, but the better you know God's voice, the more obvious Satan's counterfeit words will be."[20] The more we are immersed in God's Word, the more we will be able to discern Satan's misperception, lies, misguidance, discouragement, and bullying. In contrast, God's Spirit will give love, joy, peace, patience, kindness, goodness, faithfulness, and self-control. (See Galatians 5:22.) Even in times of correction, we will have a very *precise* command from God as to what we are to correct. God wants us to be whole and healthy. But Satan only gives us *generalities* that make us feel bad about ourselves and cause us to question God. Again, if it is not in His Word, it is not a Word from God.

Do you have any questions about God's will for your life? Do you have any tough circumstances for which you need guidance or encouragement? Are you struggling with whether something you are doing is pleasing to the Lord? Is there a *voice* you feel is speaking to you? Then dive into the Bible and seek God with all your heart and He will make His ways clear to you. Jesus said, "My sheep know my voice" (John 10:4-5; 14; 27). When God speaks, you will know it is He when you recognize Him through His Word.

And, like Elijah, when you focus on God's truth in your circumstances, you will have confidence that God will do what He says He will do in His Word, faith to claim His promises, strength to make a difference, wisdom to know His will, ears in tune to His voice, and the eyes to see God's power at work in your life!

TOO MUCH FOR YOU

WARMING UP

- Begin today by asking the Holy Spirit to speak to you through His Word.
- Please read 1 Kings 19:1-8.

ACT 4, SCENE 3

Recently I ran out of gas trying to get from one place to another in a hurry. I felt as if I didn't have time to stop until I did one more thing. But my car had a different agenda. Without gas it could not make it, no matter how much I willed it to go as it sputtered and died in the road. What made it even worse was that it was my birthday. I thought getting older made you wiser! I was only made wiser by learning the hard way that I cannot multitask on empty! We will get back to this story . . . now let's turn our attention to Elijah.

In the last couple chapters, through the power of God, Elijah has raised a child from the dead, brought fire from heaven, defeated the prophets of Baal, successfully interceded for rain after three and a half years of drought, and ran six miles from Mount Carmel to Jezreel in four minutes flat (give or take).

Elijah is about to run out of gas.

At this point it looks as if Elijah is simply running for no other reason except to get away from Jezebel. Jezebel was the queen of more than Israel; she was also the original drama queen. If there was trouble to be found, you can be sure she was not only in the middle of it, but likely the instigator. It is also pretty safe to say that she was a sore loser. Elijah had not only defeated her prophets on Mount Carmel, but he had them executed in the Kishon Valley. (We will discuss this more in week six.)

- Read verses 1-3 again and paraphrase what happened in your own words.

_____

_____

_____

Needless to say, I have seen two-year-olds more mature than Ahab. Every time someone crosses him, Ahab tattles to Jezebel. Now Elijah is on the run again . . . this time running for his life! But Elijah is running on empty.

THE SET:

- Review 1 Kings 18:46. From where is Elijah coming? Where is he now in 1 Kings 19:3-4?

_____

_____

- **Fill in the blanks below according to verse 4 (NIV):**
  "He came to a broom tree, sat down under it and prayed that _____
  _____ _____. 'I have had _____, Lord,' he said. 'Take
  my _____ . . .'"

Elijah had burned out! He showed all the symptoms: exhaustion, loneliness, depression, fear, attempts to run away from his problems. His *fiery* personality was quenched by fear and exhaustion. The "broom tree" in the above verse is also called a "juniper tree." And Elijah was having a "juniper tree moment!" As we read in last week's lesson from James 5:17, "Elijah was a man just like us." We were inspired by that comparison last week, but today we can really relate. His humanity was showing through.

- Why do you think Elijah burned out?

  _____

  _____

Due to Elijah's many recent grand ministry moments, it was likely that Elijah was not *taking in* as much as he was *giving out*. I believe that describes the majority of people I know—myself included. We are well-meaning and good-hearted about all we do for God and for others, but somehow lose our balance as we teeter between serving others and taking care of ourselves. We can become especially vulnerable to discouragement, depression, and temptation when, as we used to say in Alabama where I grew up, we are "plum wore out." I know one of my weaknesses is to jump in and volunteer every time I see a need. Even though we all need to do our fair share of helping out as needed, we must also balance that with the art of saying "no." We must first seek the guidance of the Holy Spirit to see if He is asking us to help. God does not ask us to do everything. He knows our limitations. Do we?

I have learned this the hard way more than once. The holiday season is busy for everyone and one particular year recently was no exception for me. In addition to all the parties I attended and hosted, I had added responsibilities at my children's school. I made it worse with my perfectionist personality by doing most of it without asking for help. The outcome was a frazzled and sick woman who couldn't catch her breath, literally. I was sent to a cardiologist who ran some tests and found some minor abnormalities. He informed me that I was okay, but I needed to slow down. I jokingly said that my official diagnosis was that I finally discovered that I am not Wonder Woman! Why do so many of us run ourselves in the ground before we realize that?

- **When have you had a *juniper tree moment*? When did you last feel like saying, "I have had enough, Lord!"?**

  _____

  _____

In Laurie Beth Jones's book, *Jesus Life Coach*, she speaks of practicing "planned abandonment." This is purposefully saying "no" to some opportunities so that we can better do the more important things in our lives. She says, "Planned abandonment doesn't mean walking away from something that is difficult or isn't working anymore. Planned abandonment means choosing between good and great, between better and best."[21]

I practiced planned abandonment when I chose to give up my career as a physician assistant when my children were young. It was a tough transition for me away from what I had prepared so long and hard to do, but I have never regretted my decision. I could always go back if I wanted to, but for what my family needed at the time, I chose between good and great, better and best!

- At the end of this chapter, you will have an opportunity to practice "planned abandonment," but for now list one activity you are presently doing that may not be necessary.

  _____

  _____

- **In verses 5-7 God Himself responded to Elijah's need with very practical help. What did He provide for Elijah?**

  _____

  _____

Do not discount the healing power of sleep. We often try to get by on less sleep by adding caffeine (my favorite: a tall, nonfat, peppermint mocha with a little whip). Right about now some of you may be thinking, "Okay, I get it. I'll get more rest. Just don't mess with my latte." I'll back off, but let's just remember that nothing substitutes taking care of ourselves with a good night's sleep, exercise, and eating right. My mother-in-law likes to tell about my husband getting cranky when he was little and she knew that most of the time all he needed was some food and a nap. Brent still says that cures just about everything for him even now.

That was where God started with Elijah. In fact, after one meal and a nap, the angel of the Lord came back again and said, "Get up and eat, for the journey is too much for you." And, again, Elijah ate the bread and drank the water provided by the Lord. Bread and water. It sounds plain and unexciting, doesn't it? But when Elijah was parched and famished, it brought life and fulfillment.

- **How is Jesus described in John 6:51?**

  _____

- **In John 4:10?**

  _____

Jesus brings life and fulfillment to our weary bodies and souls. Time spent with our Lord brings renewal, healing, and life. Without regular intake of the Bread of Life and The Living Water, we become dry spiritually and show signs of being malnourished, as Elijah did. This is where I fear too many of us go wrong. It seems that when life gets hectic, our quiet time with the Lord is the first thing to go. In the words of Richard J. Foster, "If we are constantly being swept off our feet with frantic activity, we will be unable to be attentive at the moment of inward silence. A mind that is harassed and fragmented by external affairs is hardly prepared for meditation."[22]

Sitting on the side of the road, out of gas and temporarily stranded, I looked down and saw the little Bible that I keep in the car. I decided this was good a time as any, so I relaxed, read some Scripture, and said a prayer. You know you are a tired mom when running out of gas is a blessing! Then the Lord's gentle whisper said, "So many times you stop short with 'I can do all things' and run yourself ragged. But Philippians 4:13 adds, 'through Christ who gives me strength.' When you fill up your spiritual gas tank by spending time with me first, I will give you the strength to carry on."

- What was Jesus's response to Martha's frantic activity in Luke 10:38-42?

_____

_____

Jesus is the One thing that is needed. To sit at His feet, like Mary, is all we need to find strength for our journeys. In the words of Dr. Hardy C. Powers, "Many of the problems we deal with are not because of being overloaded, but because of our under-being." When we give more than we receive spiritually, we run the risk of running dry. But God wants to strengthen us for our journeys through the Bread of Life and Living Water. Nothing else will satisfy.

Will you join me and let some less important things go for now? Let's choose between good and great, better and best, and make time to sit at Jesus's feet. Only He can fill our cups to overflowing!

- Practice a time of planned abandonment. Make two lists below, one list labeled "DO NOT DISTURB," which are your priorities in life. The second list will be labeled "ELIMINATE," which are distractions.

    1. _____
       _____
       _____
       _____
       _____
       _____

    2. _____
       _____
       _____
       _____
       _____
       _____

BEING STILL

WARMING UP

- Begin today by asking the Holy Spirit to speak to you through His Word.
- Please read 1 Kings 19:8.

ACT 4, SCENE 4

THE SET:

Now picture the scenery changing rapidly as Elijah travels from Jezreel to Beersheba to the hot, arid landscapes of the desert. Imagine the fear in Elijah's eyes as he turns to look over his shoulder to see if anyone is following him. See Elijah's slumped shoulders and dragging feet from exhaustion, thirst, and depression. But he also has a look of determination on his face. He is not giving up yet.

- In verse 8, how long is Elijah's journey?

  _____

- What is his destination?

  _____

- **Why is Mount Horeb also called the "mountain of God"? What is another name for Mount Horeb? Please read Exodus 19:1-2; 10; 23.**

  _____

  _____

His journey is long, but Elijah has a goal. He has set his sights on Mount Horeb as an unconventional place to vacation: an oasis in the desert, literally and figuratively, for his weary body and soul. Mount Horeb is Mount Sinai, the very place God met with Moses centuries earlier, the location where God gave Moses the Ten Commandments and all the laws of Israel and instructions for the tabernacle, and allowed Moses to see Him as He passed by. "So, what starts as flight from Jezebel's wrath takes on the character of pilgrimage to the places of his very roots."[23] Elijah found his sanctuary.

- How would you define a *sanctuary*?

  _____

- On a scale of 1-10, how much do you prioritize corporate worship with fellow believers in your church sanctuary?

  _____

  _____

- Whisper a prayer right now asking God to help you prioritize corporate worship with other believers at church and ask Him to help you go *expecting* an encounter with Him.

For me, a sanctuary is any place where God draws us back to a place of worship where He is waiting to meet with us. It is common for churches to be called "sanctuaries" because it is a designated place where we *expect* an encounter with God. In addition to our corporate worship in our church sanctuaries, we also need a very personal place of worship. Elijah left his servant behind before he took his journey to Mount Horeb. He needed to be alone with the Lord. He needed some answers and a refuge. He needed a personal encounter with God!

Like Elijah, we also need to find our own personal sanctuary where we go to meet with the Lord on a regular basis. It can be a quiet walk outside (my personal favorite); time with the Lord in the morning before the rush of the day; meditation and prayer while gardening; a big, comfy chair and a cup of coffee with your Bible; or a quiet drive enjoying the vastness of the sky and the bigness of God. (Obviously the latter would be while the children are not in the car!) For my husband, it is a deer stand. I love sending him on a hunting trip because he returns renewed and inspired after communing with God in the beauty of His creation.

- **What is your favorite personal sanctuary?**

_____

_____

This leads us to our fourth way to prepare our hearts to hear the voice of the Lord:

PREP STEP # 4: BEING STILL

Being still is, in essence, the other half of prayer. Our ACTIVE prayer is when we come to God with our praise, thanksgivings, confession, and requests. Being still before God is RECEPTIVE prayer. Listening. Allowing the Holy Spirit to speak to us. It is an attitude of prayer. A posture that is ready to receive. It is a time when we are focused on the Lord and not on what He can do for us.

Sometimes being still is referred to as "meditation." But let's clarify this word first.

- What do you think of when you hear the word "meditation"?

_____

_____

I absolutely loved it recently when my boys woke up one morning and jumped in my bed and just wanted to snuggle. This was priceless to me because they weren't asking for chocolate milk or waffles or to turn on the television. They just wanted to be with me. Don't you imagine that is the way our Heavenly Father feels when we just want to be in His presence, not asking anything of Him except to know Him better? That is meditation: listening, applying God's Word to our lives, being still in His presence.

Being still is actually an oxymoron. "Still" in this sense is not to stay motionless. As I said above, I am often best at *being still* before God when I am walking. Those of us who have ADD tendencies may find it hard to be still, but we can be moving and still quiet our hearts. "What happens in meditation is that we create the emotional and spiritual space that allows Christ to construct an inner *sanctuary* in the heart."[24] It is during those times of stillness that I am in tune to the Holy Spirit and He brings to my mind thoughts of His glory, new revelations and understanding of Scripture, even practical insights into my day, and reminders of His love for me.

"Meditation is God's invitation to take his Word seriously."[25] First, we spend time with God in *prayer* and study His Word. Then, in moments of *stillness* we allow God to speak to us and apply His Word to our lives. As we *obey* what we hear Him saying to us, we continue to construct a place of sanctuary in our hearts in which the Holy Spirit dwells. These PREP STEPS work together to prepare our hearts to be a place God is welcome to reside and receptive to hear Him speak.

Now, let's look at a couple additional benefits of *being still* before the Lord:

1.   Stillness = Rest/Renewal

I can tell the difference when I have not "been still" in a while. So can those around me (just ask my husband and kids). I feel more anxious, fretful, and edgy. Like Elijah, we can become defeated, depressed, and a real bummer to be around when we do not stop to drink in the healing presence of God. Elijah was running from his problems, albeit BIG problems, like a threat on his life . . . but running nonetheless.

Sometimes we feel like we are running for our lives because of issues or problems that we face. But most often we are just running *because* of life. Life gets so busy that we feel like we can't keep up—but we can't slow down either. When I find myself in this state of chaos physically, I can almost always expect it to affect me spiritually. I may start the race on track with God, but somewhere along the way I get off course when the load gets too heavy. I am sometimes tempted to lighten my load by throwing off precious time with the Lord, but have learned that my strength comes from Him alone. When I prioritize time alone with God, I am never disappointed!

- Do you have trouble prioritizing time with the Lord when things get hectic?

  _____

- Write a time here when you will spend time with God in prayer and Bible study each day:

  _____

  _____

2.   Stillness = Seeing the greatness of God

Elijah's problem was that his view of his problems became bigger than his view of God. That's what happens when we focus on ourselves and on our circumstances instead of fastening our gaze upon the source of our help and strength.

  a) By ourselves: Our problems are *big* and our view of God is *small*.

- Why do you suppose many people try to make it on their own without God?

  _____

  _____

For some, it may be defiant to do what they want instead of obeying God's commands, but for many it is daily frustrations, society's pressures, and busyness that narrow their view of God. Unfortunately, the result of doing so is that many people settle for a life of anxiety, bitterness, and a general lack of joy. I think it must be that last symptom listed that may grieve God most—our lack of joy. His heart must ache when He sees us settle for less than His best for us. I want to shout out to everyone and say, "It can be so much better than this! The Lord has brought me so much joy! And I know that is what the Lord wants for you too. Passion and joy in your relationship with God can spill over into every area of your life!"

b) In God's presence: Our problems are *small* and our view of God is *big*.

- **Finish Psalm 46:10 in the space below:**
  "_____ _____, and _____ that I am _____."
- **In your own words, what is the OPPOSITE of this verse?**

  _____
  _____

- **Why is it so important to be still and know that He is God right now for you?**

  _____
  _____

He will be God whether or not we acknowledge Him. In her Bible study, *Believing God*, Beth Moore states, "all attempts to take away the mystery and wonder that surround God leave Him being pictured as something He is not. We cannot tame the Lion of Judah. There is a mystery, a wonder, and, yes, even a wildness about God we cannot take away from Him."[26] God is never-changing, but in His presence we can be changed and renewed when we still our hearts long enough to see how great He really is.

I am so relieved to know the Lord is God. It brings peace to know that He sees, He has a plan, and that He is in control. It brings hope when we look up from our limited view and see God's greatness and His unlimited power to change circumstances in our lives. He is big enough to change the unchangeable, love the unlovable, melt the hearts of the sinful, and to do the impossible! When we stand in awe of God, our spirits are hushed and peaceful, yet overflowing with worship at the same time. He is so worthy of our praise, but His presence also beckons us to just *be still*.

> *"When I come into Your presence,*
> *Past the gates of praise.*
> *Into Your sanctuary,*
> *Where we're standing face to face.*
> *I look upon Your countenance,*
> *I see the glory of Your Holy face,*
> *And I can only bow down and say . . .*
> *You are awesome in this place, Mighty God.*
> *You are awesome in this place, Abba Father*
> *You are worthy of all praise,*
> *To You our lives we raise.*
> *You are awesome in this place, Mighty God."*
> *-Awesome in this place by Dave Billingham* © 1992 Integrity's Hosanna! Music / ASCAP /

SPEAKING OF LOVE

WARMING UP

- Begin today by asking the Holy Spirit to speak to you through His Word.
- Please read 1 Kings 19:9-11.

ACT 4, SCENE 5

As we continue the topic of *being still*, today we will introduce the fourth CRITERIA used for discerning God's voice. It is important to recognize the difference between our own voice, the input of others, Satan's lies and deceitfulness—and God's voice.

- What was CRITERIA #1?
  _____

- What was CRITERIA #2?
  _____

- What was CRITERIA #3?
  _____

CRITERIA #4 for discerning God's voice: WHEN GOD SPEAKS IT WILL BE IN CONTEXT OF HIS LOVE

This CRITERIA goes hand in hand with the topic of *being still* because it is during those times of stillness that we hear God speak his words of love softly and tenderly to our hearts. As we have studied in previous lessons, sometimes He has to correct us when He speaks to us, but it is always because of His love for us that He does so.

- Please read Hebrews 12:5-6. Who does the Lord discipline?
  _____

- **What was Elijah's fear in verse 10?**
  _____

- **In the midst of one of Elijah's lowest moments of fear and fatigue, what did the Lord say to him in verse 11?**
  _____
  _____

Elijah had seen the power of God displayed through miracles and answered prayers, but now he just needed to experience the power of God through His presence. Elijah had been so busy running for his life that he had not stopped to inquire of the Lord the truth of his situation . . . until now. And now Elijah was ready to listen.

All around us God is trying to get our attention . . . preferably through the beauty of His creation, through the love of others, in times of prayer, and in the pages of Scripture brought to life in us through the Holy Spirit. But He will also use our tough circumstances to speak to us. He is willing to teach us the lessons we need to learn to help us reach maturity. But most of all He wants to teach us that He is all we need.

To know Him and His love is more important than all the mysteries of heaven. Just think . . . everything from creation to Revelation, just to have a relationship with you. Every act of mercy, grace, compassion, and forgiveness . . . just to demonstrate His love. He is incapable of anything less. After giving His only Son, how could He do more?

In our times of trial, God is passing close by, ready to gently whisper to our hearts. When God speaks to us, it is not so much for us to know more *about* Him as it is for us to *know* Him. The central theme of the Bible is God reaching down to man to draw us closer to Him. He uses people, circumstances, His Word, His voice, and His Son just to tell us, "I LOVE YOU!" If we fail to grasp that, we fail to see His heart. It is why He created you and died for you and continues to pursue you. *He loves you.*

- Let that soak in for a minute. Stop right now, close your eyes and let the Holy Spirit envelope you and speak God's great love for you.
- What did you sense the Lord saying to you? Is it hard for you to accept His love?

_____

_____

_____

Today we will look up several Scriptures. When we are discovering God's great love for us, I would much rather you hear His words to you instead of mine. I encourage you to look up each Scripture and let God's words of love for you soak into your heart, mind, and soul.

- Summarize how God shows His love for you in each Scripture below:
  1. Psalms 139:1-18

  _____

  _____

  2. Jeremiah 29:11

  _____

  _____

  3. Isaiah 49:15-16

  _____

  _____

  4. Ephesians 2:4-5

  _____

  _____

5. Ephesians 3:17-19

   _____

   _____

6. Colossians 3:12

   _____

   _____

- **Now put a star by the Scripture(s) that specifically spoke to you today. What is your response to these love letters from God to you?**

   _____

   _____

   _____

One morning recently, it seemed that everything I did was enveloped in praise: I woke with a prayer on my lips, tackled my to-do list with a song in my heart, and still had time for a walk. Believe me, this is *unusual*. Most days I just wish I didn't have to wake up! I don't know what makes some days different than others, but I think God had something up His Almighty sleeve. As I walked a different route than usual, it opened up to the most beautiful path along a river that I had never seen before. It was like a little present for me that God couldn't wait for me to find. It may not sound like much to you, but for me it was a sanctuary as we discussed this week, and I felt His presence so close. I knew He had been waiting to meet me there. Oh, that God would care about my smallest desires blew me away!

I believe that spending time *being still* with God that morning had primed my heart to experience Him and sense His voice directing me toward this special meeting place He had for us. The funny thing was that the Lord didn't have anything new to tell me. When I got there, God had no revelation of profound, hidden truths waiting for me. I just became acutely aware of God's greatness and of His great love for me. That's all He wanted to say. That's all I needed to hear.

After that walk I was so aware that God had passed by that I came home and penned these words:

> *Lord, You still amaze me.*
>
> *I see Your love in the majesty of a sunrise and in the trillions of stars lighting up the night. I know You are Creator of all when I hear the cry of a newborn baby, feel my husband's loving touch, smell a rose, and see the fingers of my son.*
>
> *You overwhelm me with how personal Your love can be; right where we are most broken is where You pour it out. You poured Your love on a tired woman by the well. It became sight for the blind man and legs for the crippled. The same love that drew children to Your side forgave the thief on the cross.*

I'll never get over the fact that You chose to leave the throne of heaven to become the servant of man. That you chose love instead of hate. Humility instead of pride. Grace instead of judgment. And that when You chose the cross . . . You chose me.

I'll never get over it. You still amaze me!

Don't miss out on what God also has up His Almighty sleeve for you. Today's lesson is a little shorter because I want you to spend some time *being still* before the Lord. Bask in His presence, sing His praises, bear your soul, and hear Him say, "I LOVE YOU!"

- Your assignment for today is some *eco-therapy* (aka get outside). Just soak in His love for you and worship His greatness as you go for a walk together (for as long or short as fits your schedule). Then write what your time of stillness with Him meant to you. (Be ready to share this experience with your small group this week if you feel comfortable doing so.)

ACT 5

A VOICE FROM THE UPPERSTAGE

SCENE 1: REALITY CHECK

SCENE 2: EARTH, WIND, AND FIRE

SCENE 3: GENTLE WHISPERS

SCENE 4: ENTER: ELISHA

SCENE 5: THE GREAT I AM

REALITY CHECK

WARMING UP

- Begin today by asking the Holy Spirit to speak to you through His Word.
- Please read 1 Kings 19:9-10; 13-14.

ACT 5, SCENE 1

We have traveled with Elijah through many highs and lows on his journey thus far, but none of the highs compares to the mountaintop experience he is about to have with the Lord. When we last saw Elijah, he was enjoying some heavenly bread and water and getting some much needed shut-eye. Now, "strengthened by that food, he traveled forty days and forty nights until he reached Horeb, the mountain of God" (v. 8). Finally, after forty days, Elijah went into a cave and spent the night.

Elijah did not come to Mount Horeb, the mountain of God, by mistake. You don't just travel forty days and forty nights to a sacred place—a holy ground—for nothing. Elijah needed some answers. He was having a pity-party and God was invited. Jezebel was still on her rampage, and Elijah was scared to death.

The Questions of God

- **In verse 9, what did God ask Elijah?**

  _____

  _____

- **What was Elijah's answer? Fill in the blanks below according to verse 10 (NIV): "He replied, 'I have been very _____ for the LORD God Almighty. The _____ have rejected your covenant, broken down your _____, and put your _____ to _____with the sword. I am the _____ _____ _____, and now they are trying to _____ me too.'"**

Elijah wanted some answers, but instead God chose to ask him some questions.

- Look over verses 9-13 again. How many times did God ask Elijah the same question?

  _____

- Look at Elijah's response in verses 10 and 14. Are his responses the same or different?

  _____

  _____

Elijah's response is exactly the same both times, and it even seems a little rehearsed. Every word is the same as if he memorized his answer. It reminds me of when I know I am wrong about something that I know I need to explain. I try to think ahead of time how to word it so that I don't look quite as guilty. Is it just me or do we all do that?

Elijah was strengthened by the angel of the Lord for his journey. Evidently God intended to send Elijah somewhere, so why did God ask Elijah, "Why are you here, Elijah?" when he showed up at Mount Horeb? Maybe Elijah was supposed to be somewhere else. Maybe God was just pointing out the obvious—that Elijah was running from something. But God specializes in turning our detours into Divine destinations. Instead of chastising Elijah, God listened to him and made sure Elijah received what he came for . . . an encounter with God!

A question makes you stop and think. That is why I ask you questions in our Bible study. Instead of only reading what I say, you are asked to engage in the study, discover the meaning of God's Word for yourself and learn to apply it to your own life. So, on that note, let me ask you:

- **Why do *you* think God asked Elijah the question, "What are you doing here, Elijah?"**

_____

_____

Check, Please!

Elijah's answer to God's question was quite exaggerated. Some of his fears were true, but some of them had been blown out of proportion. Elijah told God that he was the only one left who was still true to God.

- Is that the truth according to verse 18?

_____

- How many had not bowed down to Baal?

_____

I think Elijah needed a reality check. I have needed a few of those from time to time, haven't you? Some reality checks are a tough pill to swallow, but sometimes they are quite funny when they come straight from the mouth of babes.

I was surprised by my son, Matthew, then seven years old, when he spoke up from the backseat of the car. He said, "Mommy, you look pretty today." Startled and tenderly amused, I replied, "Well, thank you, Matthew." He added, "You get prettier every day." *How sweet. He really takes after his father.* But then he went on . . . "Yeah, you're medium pretty." *Excuse me?* Not knowing he should stop while he was ahead, he continued, "You know what that means, Mommy?" *Oh, I can't wait to hear this.* "That means you aren't super pretty, but you're not ugly." *Reality check!* I wasn't feeling particularly proud before the "compliment," but I sure had a new dose of humility when it was over. Well, I guess a backhanded compliment is still a compliment!

All joking aside, some of my reality checks have also come from serious circumstances. When my children are going to the doctor for the millionth time, it seems, I can't help but feel a little sorry for them (and myself) that they have had so much to deal with in their young lives. But it never fails that right about the time I want to cry out, "Oh Lord, why them? Why me?" I see a child wheeled by in a wheelchair with no hair and an IV filled with chemotherapy. Shame on me for ever complaining even one time to God about this blessed life that I live. There will always be someone in better shape or worse shape than me, and I must be grateful for all God has done in my situation.

It's easy to get so spoiled, isn't it? We are tempted to complain about the car that only has 100,000 miles on it, the house that only has two bathrooms, and that the grocery store is "all the way in town." Then we turn on one of our many televisions to see adults and children that walk with no shoes, live in a hut made out of boxes in a garbage dump, and who think that *any* food would be worth finding just to keep them alive. It's all too easy to let things in life get out of perspective.

- **Do you sometimes need a reality check? If so, when?**

———————————————————————————————————

———————————————————————————————————

We really do have legitimate problems to deal with, but we must keep them in God's perspective, not ours. We cannot see what He sees and know what He knows. He knows what we can handle and what we cannot. He knows what pruning we need and how we can mature and gain character. He knows what is best for His kingdom. Our all-knowing God knows what is best for us and promises to work everything for our good, according to His timing and His will, if we are in Christ Jesus. (See Jeremiah 29:11.)

Like Elijah, do you sometimes feel like saying, "I have been very zealous for the LORD God Almighty, but—" . . . "I try to make a difference and nothing happens" . . . "No one carries this kind of load" . . . "I am running for my life and I can't keep up!"? Hear the LORD say to you, "Why are you here, _____? Why are you discouraged? Why are you running from your problems? Why are you so worried? Why are you in this place of denial of my ability to handle this for you?" We may come looking for answers, but God wants to ask us some questions. He wants us to place our realities at His feet so He can redefine them.

On our family vacation to Disney World, I noticed that the attractions were designed to redefine reality. The rides make you feel like you are really underwater, on the safari, or visiting Never Land. Obviously my surroundings were not what I perceived them to be. I needed a *reality check* to remember that I was not really flying uncontrollably at two Gs into outer space!

- What seems bigger to you than it really is and you would like to see it from God's perspective?

———————————————————————————————————

———————————————————————————————————

We must let God redefine our realities. Things are not always as large as they appear! We may perceive our surroundings as out of control, but God is very much in control! Let God give you peace by placing what bothers you at His feet and leaving it there. Then focus on His greatness, His power, and His care for you. It is actually faith in God that moves our mountains—not our faith in ourselves. That's good news, wouldn't you say?

- **Now it gets exciting! Please read aloud verse 11.**

Elijah was in a cave, literally but also figuratively. He saw his world as dark, gloomy, and full of despair. But God invited him to step out of his disillusionment and into a fresh perspective of truth and hope.

There is no need to worry and every reason to praise because the Lord is passing by! There is hope in desperation. God is able to use those moments when reality hits us between the eyes as a wake-up call. He wants to remind us that He is close to us in times of trouble and that there is nothing that He cannot handle if we will trust Him. When we are in our caves of needless worry and despair, God calls to us by name. Then He invites us to step out of the shadows and into His presence.

EARTH, WIND, AND FIRE!

WARMING UP

- Begin today by asking the Holy Spirit to speak to you through His Word.
- Please read 1 Kings 19:11-12.

ACT 5, SCENE 2

Life is so busy! Between sharing a home with three men (two of whom are still young enough to have cartoons on their pj's), being a pastor's wife, directing a local food pantry, volunteering at the kids' school, shuttling to ball games and choir practice, writing, helping with homework, running errands, and being somewhat of a "blonde" (I can say it—you can't!), there is plenty of chaos in my life! But I know I'm not alone.

- What about you? What is on your to-do list that makes your life busy? (Add more lines in the margin if you need to!)

_____

_____

Unfortunately, my multitasking can lead to a few mishaps. In fact, instead of crying over my many blunders, I decided to laugh at them. I started making a list of all the funny things that have happened due to being over extended much of the time. Here are just a few:

You know you're a stressed-out mom when . . .

1. The only bandage you can find for yourself in the house has superheroes on it.
2. You reach out to hold another lady's hand when crossing the street while out shopping.
3. You start to cut up your husband's meat on his plate.
4. You run out of gas on the side of the road and consider it a nice break.
5. You are so exhausted after caring for your sick child who happened to throw up in the car, you forget you left the doors open in your car after cleaning it all up. Then a storm comes that pours sheeting rain into the car for two hours, ruining the DVD player in the dashboard.
6. You have to get an MRI and it is the best nap you have had in a long time.
7. At the checkout counter you cannot reach your wallet until you pull a big, plastic toy out of your purse even though no kids are with you.
8. While at a women's conference, you realize you forgot to put on deodorant that morning in your rush to get there, and the only thing you can find is some hairspray in your purse, so you spray the hairspray in your armpits!
9. You send an email to all the women in your church to sign up for the women's conference, but in your rush you forget to proofread the email. Only later do you

realize you sent this message: "Contact the front office to SIN UP before the conference!"

10. But at least I'm not the only one. My friend, Amy, is the mother of a four-year-old little girl, so dress-up parties are not unusual at her house. One day she went to check the mail at her house and waved to her neighbor as they passed by. She was feeling good about being so friendly until she remembered that she was still wearing a princess tiara on her head.

- **For Elijah in verses 11-12, what three elements were present to make his surroundings quite chaotic?**

_____

_____

Hearing God in the midst of chaos:

Like us, Elijah was also distracted by his surroundings. When God invited Elijah to step out of his cave of self-pity and into His presence, Elijah was bombarded by some harsh elements first. Elijah weathered a wind so fierce that it tore the mountains apart and shattered the rocks. That is some kind of tornado! Living in Oklahoma and Kansas has helped me understand the magnitude of this verse. One time we saw a two-funnel F-5 tornado from our kitchen window. It was huge and destroyed everything in its path. Yet I don't think that even an F-5 tornado can tear a mountain apart. Then Elijah withstood an earthquake. Devastation, loss, and fear was about all that was left the after the 2010 earthquakes in Haiti. Pictures of the lost and terrified faces of the Haitians will forever be imprinted on my mind. I don't know how Elijah felt when the earthquake came, but I imagine his reaction was much the same. Elijah then braved a fire, in which the dense smoke would make it difficult to see and breathe, and the intense heat surely made it almost too hot to bear.

Yet even as these powerful elements swept by, Elijah knew it was not God. *Elijah had to discern God's voice in the midst of the chaos.*

Our turbulent surroundings can place us at risk of not hearing God's voice clearly. *Earthquakes* are things that distract us and cause us to focus on our problems and ourselves more than God. It may be hard to see Him at work through the smoke of the *fires* we are trying to put out around us. These fires can seem to need our immediate attention instead of giving God the time he deserves. Or it may be difficult at times to discern His voice from the noisy *winds* around us, such as the media, our friends, or family, and a constant source of technology always within our reach.

- **Do you have any *earthquakes, winds,* or *fires* (aka, chaos) distracting you from hearing the Lord?**

_____

_____

Sometimes God speaks through extraordinary circumstances, but more often our circumstances can distract us from hearing His voice. Our task is to stay so in tune with God that we can discern when God is speaking in the midst of the chaos.

Hearing God in the midst of the storm:

There is a difference between *chaos* and the *storms of life*. Chaos threatens to distract us, whereas the *storms of life* try to overtake us. Storms tend to be more dramatic and life changing than everyday chaos. Storms can be brewing in the distance for a while and gradually wear us down, or they can form suddenly and unexpectedly, turning our lives upside down. These storms can come in the form of divorce, death, serious illness, depression, and danger . . . just to name a few.

- **What storms are you facing now or have you weathered in the past?**

_____

_____

I have a sweet friend who recently went through a couple difficult years with her husband, ending in divorce. At times she wondered how she could make it one more day emotionally, physically, or financially. To be honest, at times I also wondered how she could cope. But I saw her grow closer to the Lord during that time due to sheer desperation. She found Him in her storm. Her faith in God and what she can handle together with Him matured, and her walk with Him became a beautiful part of her life.

I have another friend who is a recovered alcoholic. She is a beautiful example of a prodigal child come home. She has become an amazing woman of God who has a hunger and thirst for God that is contagious. She inspires me more than she knows. Recently she told me of a rough week she was having at work. She said that in the years prior to her rededication to Christ, a week like that would have had her drunk every night. Then, with tears in her eyes, she said, "But I don't need it anymore. I have peace and I am okay." God was with her during her storm.

- **Look back at verse 11 and fill in the blanks: "then a great and powerful wind tore the mountains apart and shattered the rocks _____ _____ _____ . . ." (NIV).**

"Before the Lord" implies that these things were happening as God was watching: God chose to later reveal Himself to Elijah in a different way, but He was with Elijah through every crashing quake, thrashing wind, and scorching fire.

It seems that we cling to God the hardest when the winds threaten to blow us over, the waves try to drown us, and the fires start to burn. Praise God, we are not alone in our strife. God is in the storm! Elijah may not have been able to hear Him while the storms raged by, but God was there with him the whole time. "What a wonderful thought, when the storms of life are all about us, we have God standing by."[27] We may not always be able to recognize God's presence when we are knee-deep in the mire of life, but He is not only there with us, He is holding us tightly so that we will not be swept away.

- Write 2 Corinthians 4:16-17 in your own words.

_____

_____

_____

- Finish this verse from Philippians 4:7 (NIV):
  "And the _____ of God, which _____ all _____,
  will guard your hearts and your minds in Christ Jesus."

We are given a peace that actually guards our hearts and our minds from the harsh elements that threaten to steal our sense of security. In Christ Jesus we have a shield of peace to face the known and the unknown.

It may be hardest to praise God in the midst of the storm, but our job is to praise in the good times, to be moldable in the hard times, and trust in uncertain times. When we do this, our faith grows stronger and our lives become a testimony to those around us of the grace of God in the midst of circumstances that threaten to overtake us.

- Look up John 16:22 and write it below, inserting your name in the place of *you and your*:
  _____
  _____
  _____

My prayer is that no matter what you face, you will know that God is standing close by, making sure that you are not swept away by life's storms. And I pray that you will have a peace that passes understanding and a joy that this world cannot take away. And whether God chooses to reveal Himself to you during your storm or in a gentle whisper after He has calmed and quieted you . . . remember that He has never left your side.

GENTLE WHISPERS

WARMING UP

- Begin today by asking the Holy Spirit to speak to you through His Word.
- Please read 1 Kings 19:13.

ACT 5, SCENE 3

THE SET:

- **Where is Elijah in today's Scripture reading?**

_____

Yesterday we saw how God is with us in our storms even though we may not always be able to recognize Him. Today we have the privilege of listening in as God chooses to reveal Himself in an intimate and personal way to Elijah. Even more amazing is that we are also invited to join this tender moment and listen as God whispers our name. Imagine, the God of the Universe—who knows all things, sees all things, can do all things, and created all things—sees you and sees me and bends down close to speak to us.

God is all around us, working in our lives, our churches, and in our world to bring as many as will let Him to a saving knowledge of Jesus Christ. We expect God to reveal His presence in revivals, church services, conferences, and rallies. And we are not surprised when He speaks to our pastor, speaker, or highly visible spiritual leaders. But do we always expect to hear God's voice or even know how to recognize His voice in our own lives?

- The thing that confuses me most about listening to God is . . .

_____

_____

Elijah could have assumed the flashy environment (earthquake, winds, and fire) he found himself in was where God would naturally be found since God is so great and powerful. God has and can reveal Himself in this way. (See Deuteronomy 4:33 and Exodus 3:4.) But the beauty and mystery of God Almighty is that He also speaks through quiet moments as well. Had Elijah not known His Father's voice, he could have missed it completely—mistaking the spectacular for the Spirit, mistaking emotion for the Almighty.

God can _show up_ any way He chooses, but, praise God, He chooses to reveal Himself in the most intimate and personal way possible for each of us! If we only look for Him in the dramatic or spectacular, we chance missing out on the relationship.

But there is a catch: Unless we are preparing our hearts to become more sensitive to God's voice, we will most likely not hear Him, even in the most dramatic of circumstances.

- **Test question: How do we prepare our hearts to hear God's voice *every day*? (Hint: the four PREP steps.)**

    1. _____

    2. _____

    3. _____

    4. _____

At the risk of sounding redundant, I want to drill these concepts into our heads so that we can refer to them at any point in our days when we are wondering why we may not be sensing God's voice. I know I use them personally as a gauge for my spiritual journey. Just like a checkpoint in an airport for our luggage, we can use these prep steps as an X-ray of our souls to see if we are on the right track.

- According to verse 12, what did God's voice sound like to Elijah?

    _____

    _____

- How did Elijah respond in verse 13?

    _____

In the RSV (Revised Standard Version) the "gentle whisper" of God is translated as a "still, small voice." Literally, the Hebrew meaning is "a voice, a fine (barely audible) whisper."[28] God rarely shouts. Usually He speaks to us through moments in our days that seem ordinary at first glance. But a tendered, sensitive heart will hear His voice and recognize that it is the Lord, turning our ordinary days into extraordinary moments!

We can look for the divine in the ordinary during our times of personal prayer, moments of stillness with the Lord, and while reading God's Word. But a sensitive heart to the Lord may also encounter Him while listening to a song that speaks to your heart, through a sermon, or during a conversation with a godly friend. I especially hear the Lord speaking through His Word, but I have sensed God speaking to me more than once through things my children say or do and through the wise counsel of my husband.

- In what way does God usually to speak to you?

    _____

    _____

This lesson today is especially dear to me. It was from this concept of *gentle whispers* that God birthed the idea for this Bible study. I noticed that God would speak to me in the midst of the chaos in my life. That reminded me of Elijah hearing the gentle whisper of God in the midst of the chaos around him. Then, as I read Elijah's story, I *really* began to hear God speak. The Lord began to pour out spiritual insights so fast that I could hardly keep up. His gentle whispers *blew me away*! God wants to do the same in all of us. He wants to blow us away with the depth of His love for us and incredible revelations of Who He is and insights into His Word.

- **What does God want us to understand when He speaks to us? (Use Ephesians 3:17-19 and Philippians 1:9-11 to help guide your answer.)**

_____

_____

_____

In addition to God's "still, small voice" or "gentle whisper," it is also recorded in Revelation 1:15 and Ezekiel 43:2 that God's voice is like the sound of "rushing waters." But God's voice is not always audible. He probably knows that we would faint dead on the spot, have a car wreck, or embarrass ourselves in front of strangers asking, "Did you hear that? I think I just heard the Lord!" It wouldn't be the first time I have been the recipient of some crazy looks!

Certainly God has spoken audibly in history, but He also speaks using many other methods. In these days of the New Testament, God uses the Holy Spirit to speak to us (Acts 2:4). For us, the "still, small voice" of God is the Holy Spirit guiding us, correcting us, and teaching us the things of God through His Word. When we can stay in tune with the frequency of the Holy Spirit, we learn to recognize His promptings so that when He speaks to us, there is no doubt that it is the Lord!

- **One time I was sure God was speaking to me was . . .**

_____

_____

Experiencing God's voice creates a passion inside to which nothing else compares. Elijah knew this passion. He had experienced God's presence in miraculous ways. Elijah had witnessed healings and provisions and fire from heaven. He had seen God's deliverance and he had seen God's wrath. Elijah knew the power of God in the storms, earthquakes, winds, and fires, and he knew the power of God in just a whisper. What was the result? Elijah *knew* God and had a passion for the Lord lit inside like fire from heaven.

As we walk with God, we come to know His voice and, best of all, we come to know Him! We experience God when we receive His healing, provisions, answers to prayer, peace during our storms, and gentle whispers in our days. What is the result? Our hearts will burn within us as God lights a passion in us for Him. (See Luke 24:13-32.)

Seek Him with all your heart and He will be found. Nothing else compares!

- Look back over some of the notes you have written throughout this study so far. Look for ways that you have felt God speaking to you through the Scriptures or the Bible study and note it below. If you are not sure if God is speaking to you, find a pastor or a godly friend to help you discern His voice.

_____

_____

_____

_____

_____

ENTER: ELISHA

WARMING UP

- Begin today by asking the Holy Spirit to speak to you through His Word.
- Please read 1 Kings 19:15-18.

ACT 5, SCENE 4

Elijah has had a big week. Let's take a few minutes to recap some of the main points we have learned from his story in the past few days.

1. God Listens:

Elijah was depressed, exhausted, angry, afraid, and lonely. God knew he needed to talk. So the Lord got the conversation started with, "What are you doing here, Elijah?" and Elijah quickly spilled his heart out to God. When we are upset, it always feels better to talk about it, doesn't it? I know, as a woman, I always feel better after talking. It is sometimes hard for my husband to understand that I can be so upset about something and then, after talking about it, immediately feel better. All my problems do not have to be solved. Sometimes I just need to be heard. God is always ready to lend us a listening ear and a shoulder to cry on.

- Are you more of a talker or a listener?

  _____

- In what situations is it important for you to feel heard?

  _____

  _____

2. God Speaks:

After Elijah was through crying out to God, I wonder if God wanted to hand Elijah a tissue and say, "Okay now, all better?" Sometimes it does feel better to talk about it, but God can do even better than that. He has answers and He wants to speak to us.

When Brent and I have an argument (yes, we all have them!), he says that he can always tell when I *am* and when I *am not* ready to listen. Usually I go through a period of wanting to be heard first. Then, after a little while, I am ready to listen to Brent's side of the story. When we are ready to listen, God has something to say that is worth listening to. He has insights and answers that we cannot see on our own. After a little while it is in our best interest to stop our ranting and raving to hear His side of the story. We might be surprised at His solutions.

3. God's Solutions:

God provided for Elijah's immediate and long-term needs. God provided for Elijah's immediate exhaustion and hunger with rest, food, and water. God provided for Elijah's frustration, fear, and anger by listening. Then God spoke to reveal His long-term solution for Elijah's depression, loneliness, and burnout.

- **According to verse 16, what was God's long-term answer for Elijah?**

ENTER STAGE RIGHT: ELISHA

When the angel of the Lord told Elijah, "This is too much for you" (v. 7), he not only meant the long journey, but also the demands of ministry. No one should attempt to do it alone. After all, it was not Elijah's ministry; it was God's ministry through Elijah. Elijah had obediently played the leading role in God's plan, and although his role was pivotal to the story, God also had someone else in mind who would play the coveted supporting role. The award for best supporting actor is a great honor for anyone in the entertainment business. Without this person, the story would be bland and boring and maybe there would be no story to tell without their encouragement to keep going, their listening ear, and their willingness to help wherever or however needed. This award could easily be named "The Elisha Award."

In reply to Elijah's complaint that he was "the only one left," God showed him very tangibly that he was not alone. He sent Elijah a ministry partner—Elisha.

- According to verse 18, how many others were still serving the Lord?

It is important to remember that ministry is not just for full-time preachers. It is for all Christians who have been called to share the good news of Jesus Christ with the world in which we live. We are a "priesthood of believers" (1 Pet. 2:9) and each of us has been given a very important task in the kingdom of God. But we were never meant to do it alone or in our own strength or resources. God will provide for our immediate needs with all of His abundant resources to equip, His presence to empower, and His Spirit to guide.

CAUTION! EXTREMELY IMPORTANT REMINDER!

We cannot get the three steps mentioned above out of order! It is of utmost importance to seek God *first* with our problems and then let Him speak His solutions to us before we go to others for help. It is too easy to pick up the phone every time we face a problem or have a complaint. God has surely given us special people in our lives to share the highs and lows of life, but we can quickly wear out those around us if we continue to dump out our laundry on them every time it gets dirty! Our friends may desire to *part* with us instead of *partner* with us!

- **Do you typically want to talk to someone when you are upset or overwhelmed? If so, who?**

- **Please look up Matthew 6:33. When you seek God first, what are you given?**

There are few blessings greater than friends and family. They are part of God's answer to our prayers and sent to encourage and bless us. But God should compete with nothing and no one for our attention. When we choose to seek the Lord first—when we turn off our cell phones, radios, televisions and computers—we will experience God in a very tender and practical way as He comes to minister to us in our time of need. I know that every time I do, He has never ceased to amaze me with His creative solutions and how personal His love can be!

- Write a prayer here asking God to help you seek Him first. Then specifically tell Him what you will not put before Him anymore. How will you trust Him to "give you all these things" as well?

THE CALL OF ELISHA

WARMING UP

- Begin today by asking the Holy Spirit to speak to you through His Word.
- Please read 1 Kings 19:19-21.

ACT 5, SCENE 5

When I first began to write this Bible study, I was encouraged to teach it at my church, even though I had not quite finished writing it yet. I had a very dear friend who saw the time crunch I was under to finish writing, typing, and preparing to teach it by a new, very quick, deadline. She came to me to ask if there was anything she could do to help. I hated to ask but recognized God's intervention. At that point I was still writing out my lessons on paper first and then typing it on the computer later. (I have mended my ways!) I was astonished to learn that she loved to type, so I handed her my rough drafts and she became my editor/secretary. Many funny memories were made as she tried to read my notes that were sometimes written up the side of a page and numbered out of sequence. But because we were focusing on the story of Elijah, it became very apparent that God had sent me my own "Elisha"—a ministry partner to share the load, to encourage, and to bless.

- **Fill in the blanks from verse 19 (NIV):**
  "So _____ went from there and found _____, son of Shaphat . . .
  Elijah went up to him and _____ his _____ around him."

"The cloak was the most important article of clothing a person could own. It was used as protection against the weather, as bedding, as a place to sit, and as luggage. It could be given as a pledge for debt or torn into pieces to show grief."[29] When Elijah threw his cloak on Elisha, it was his invitation for Elisha to join him in his service to God. *Actually, God was not only commissioning Elisha for the first time, He was also recommissioning Elijah after his burnout.*

Elijah felt helpless to be of benefit to God's kingdom any longer. He felt burned out and like yesterday's headliner instead of God's leading man. But God made sure Elijah knew He was not done with him yet. God used this mentor/apprentice, leading/supporting role relationship between Elijah and Elisha as a fresh call on Elijah's life. This commissioning of Elisha was a twofold benefit for both parties involved. It was Elisha's chance to learn from Elijah, and it was the much-needed help and encouragement Elijah needed. Win-win situation, wouldn't you say?

- Is there anyone God can use to help mentor you as you seek to serve Him?

  _____

  _____

We have all been given those that are *older* and *younger* in the faith to teach and from whom we can learn. We may not literally throw our "cloak" (i.e., our jacket) on them, but we can very literally throw our arms around them. There are many within our church walls that could use encouragement or a friend, or help serving. There are those at our places of work that need an extra spiritual nudge. And, most certainly, our own family is our responsibility and privilege to nurture in the faith.

I have played the role of Elisha and Elijah at different times. I have been very blessed to have had some precious spiritual mentors with me on my journey who played the role of Elijah for me. I have a Christian heritage, which includes my parents and grandparents on both sides of my family. But I also was given a very dear aunt who modeled a life of faith and love for Jesus. She made it fun to learn about the Bible. She had a competition for my friends and I during Vacation Bible School (many of whom were my cousins in our small church—and we were fiercely competitive!) Whoever memorized the most Bible verses won a prize. One of my first Bibles that had my name on the front came from winning one of those competitions to learn all the books of the Bible. But she also taught me how to apply God's Word to my life. She gave me a gift not only of prizes and a Bible, but treasures that have impacted my walk with Christ for the rest of my life.

In other stages of my life, I have been given other *Elijahs*. I was given a ministry role model early on in my husband's career as a pastor who helped me step out and speak before others, encouraged me to begin journaling my thoughts, and boosted my confidence in my role as a pastor's wife. And, even now, God has given me another very precious mentor in my current walk with Him to help teach me how to pray with faith, to expect miracles (which we have seen), and to be a dear friend with whom I can share my journey.

Other times I have been given the role of *Elijah*—a responsibility to mentor others in the faith. One of my favorite things to do is teach young couples. My husband and I had such a wonderful young couple's class when we were engaged and married that it has become a passion of ours to provide the same for others. Our teachers were excellent role models for us to follow. They were always well-prepared for each lesson, they listened, they cared, they provided an environment in which we could spread our wings and begin to take some leadership within God's church, and, most of all, they prayed for each one of us in the class every day and by name. Do you know what an impact that made on us to be loved and nurtured in the faith that way? We hope to somehow do the same for those that God has placed in our care.

- Does anyone come to mind that you can encourage in the faith?

Unfortunately, it is very easy to feel like we are not qualified to serve God. Satan loves to make us feel that way. There are always others that seem to do things so much better than we do. We may not feel ready or equipped or even worthy. And sometimes we try to put ourselves out to pasture before God is through with us. I know many precious saints who put themselves on the shelf because they don't feel useful in their stage of life. Maybe you are new in the faith or a beginner in your area of service, or maybe you are an empty-nester finding where you fit into God's plan again, or maybe you are getting along in years and don't feel that you have much to offer anymore. In God's timetable it does not matter what our age is, or what we feel we have done that has ruined our ministry, or if we feel that we have nothing left to offer. When we are most humble is when we are most useful.

- **Complete this verse from 1 Thessalonians 5:24 (NIV):**

  "The one who calls you is _____ and _____ will do it."

Thank the Lord, this verse does not say, "I called you, now *you* go and do it." This verse says, "*He* will do it!" We can sell ourselves so short that we walk away without our confidence. The great news is that it is not *our* confidence, but our confidence in *God* that matters most. We are called to be obedient. Period. God takes it from there. He will bless our attempts to serve Him whenever and however He sees fit. But have no doubt—He will be faithful! And He will often provide for our long-term needs of encouragement, friendship, and help through others.

- Now read verse 21 again. What did Elisha do when Elijah invited him to join him in his ministry?
  _____

- Why do you think Elisha did that?
  _____

Verse 19 says that Elisha was plowing with twelve yoke of oxen. Elisha was probably a fairly wealthy farmer to have that many oxen at hand. To kill them meant to kill his livelihood—and that's no yoke! Okay, I never was very good at punch lines. But Elisha's actions definitely showed he had no intention of turning back to his old way of life. Elisha now had a higher calling.

- **Complete this verse from Matthew 28:19: "Therefore _____ and make _____ of all nations, baptizing them in the name of the Father and the Son and the Holy Spirit, and _____ them to obey everything I have commanded you. And surely I am _____ _____ _____, to the very end of the age."**
- **What is the second word of this verse? _____!**
- **What do you feel God is calling you to "go" and do?**
  _____

  _____

- **Do you feel that you need a time of equipping and mentoring first?**
  _____

I love the quotation, "God does not call the equipped, He equips the called." The transfer of ministry from Elijah to Elisha was in motion, but before Elisha was commissioned to "go," he was allowed a time to follow. Elisha's time to lead was coming fast, but first he had much to learn. We have also been given a higher calling than to just do a job to merely exist. We are called by God to use the unique talents, gifts, and abilities He has given us to make disciples of all nations. But first we must be a disciple. We must allow God to teach us through His Word, through time spent with Him in prayer, and through other godly believers that He has placed in our path.

Then, when the time is right, we are commissioned to "go." It may seem a little scary to take that step of obedience, but when we do, we will experience the power of God at work within us. Just as a mother bird nudges her young out of the nest when it is time to fly, so God commissions us to "Go." We can trust that He is there to teach us how to spread our wings and that He will give us others that will fly alongside us.

So get ready to fly, dearly loved child of God. You were made to soar!

ACT 6

MISCUES

SCENE 1: TAKE 1, 2, 3, 4 . . .

SCENE 2: NABOTH'S VINEYARD

SCENE 3: PRIDE BEFORE THE FALL

SCENE 4: ACTING THE PART

SCENE 5: CURTAIN CALL

TAKE 1, 2, 3, 4 . . .

WARMING UP

- Begin today by asking the Holy Spirit to speak to you through His Word.
- Please read 1 Kings 20:1-43.

ACT 6, SCENE 1

I can't believe this is our last week together in this study. It has been a joy for me to share this with you. But we are not done quite yet. In our final days we will cover the last three chapters of 1 Kings fairly quickly. It will require a little more reading than we have done each day so far, but each chapter beckons us to immerse ourselves in the plot until we can picture the whole story. I am so proud of you for hanging in there until the end. But don't get faint of heart now. The finish line is just ahead, and the dramatic, inspiring ending waiting for us in God's Word will be worth the effort. So let's take our seats together on the front row again this week as the curtain rises once more to reveal a new scene.

THE SET:

In this last week of our study, Elijah disappears into the shadows for a little while as a new cast of characters are introduced and King Ahab takes the stage again. Like the old saying, "Meanwhile, back at the . . . palace," we return to the story of Ahab. We will see what Ahab did right and wrong and see how we can learn from his victories and mistakes. We have as much to learn from Ahab about what *not* to do as we learned from Elijah what we should do. In these final chapters we will see more of Ahab's highs and lows (mostly lows), and we will observe how sin blocks our spiritual ears from hearing God's voice. These "blockades" are *miscues* given to us by the enemy to throw us off from hearing truth from the Lord. Unfortunately, these miscues can grieve the heart of God and quench His Spirit from speaking in our lives. Let's do all we can to avoid the enemy's trap!

ENTER: BEN-HADAD

God used three enemies of Israel to punish them for living apart from God: Aram, Assyria, and Babylon.[30] At this time in Israel's history, Aram was an immediate threat and Ben-Hadad was Aram's arrogant and self-seeking king. It appears that Ahab has met his match. In fact, you can easily characterize Ben-Hadad as a bully. (Yep. They've always been around!) I imagine if toilets had been invented back then, he would have given Ahab a swirly! And he *did* try to steal Ahab's lunch money.

- **Look at verses 5-6. What did Ben-Hadad demand of Ahab?**

_____

_____

- Did Ahab give in to his demands in verse 9?

  _____

- What was the result in verse 12?

  _____

Ahab finally listened to some good advice from an unnamed prophet and patiently sought the word of the Lord in verses 13-30. The result was victory for Israel. But, unfortunately, his good behavior was short-lived. It seems that Ahab never learned the easy way or the hard way: the bad marriage, the idols, the consequences of sin through famine and drought, the pagan sacrifices, the warnings by prophets. And the list goes on. Imagine a movie crew shooting each scene for Ahab: Take 1, 2, 3, 4 . . . God gives Ahab second chances, and third, and fourth. We have all made wrong choices from time to time, but Ahab made the wrong choices over and over again.

- **Now look at verses 31-34 and describe what took place:**

  _____

  _____

  _____

Somethin' don't smell right! Just a few verses ago, Ben-Hadad was Ahab's enemy, but now Ahab calls him "brother." Ahab wanted territorial and commercial favors from Ben in exchange for sparing his life. Ahab knew the right thing to do, but he was willing to disobey God to get what he wanted. Dangerous choice.

Let's see where God stands on this issue.

- **Please look up Numbers 33:55. What would happen if Israel would not remove their enemies?**

  _____

  _____

- Read Psalms 106:34-39. What was the result of not obeying God's command to destroy the people of enemy nations?

  _____

  _____

- **After the battle on Mount Carmel against the prophets of Baal, what did Elijah do in 1 Kings 18:40?**

  _____

  _____

Elijah modeled the right way to handle the evil he faced. When God commanded Israel to completely get rid of evil influences, it was not to be grotesque or brutal—it was for the spiritual health of the nation. God's intention was to remove all evil influences and pagan beliefs from among the Israelites. He did not want His people to compromise their faith by mixing with idolatry. But the Israelites did not always carry out God's command to get rid of anything and anyone associated with the idolatrous nations. This led to compromise and corruption, just as God said it would, and Ahab was leading the way.

BLOCKADE #1 to hearing God's voice:
DEAFNESS DUE TO DISOBEDIENCE

Ahab was, once again, the poster child for disobedience. His life modeled what living deafened to God's voice looks like. Sin causes deafness! Ahab now had this to add to his laundry list of sins: he chose to compromise his integrity with Ben-Hadad. *Ahab chose to not hear God's voice.* He didn't want to know what God thought this time because Ahab wanted to do things his way. He wanted to take a shortcut to the top and was willing to cheat to get there. Sadly, he bypassed many victories when he failed to trust God with the direction of his life.

- Read verses 35-43 now. Here we learn Ahab's fate for his disobedience when another *unnamed prophet* approached Ahab with news of his impending punishment.
- **Please fill in the blanks from verse 42: "You have set free a man I had determined should _____. Therefore it is _____ _____ for _____ _____, your _____ for his _____."**

What began as Ahab's victory ended in defeat. We must learn from Ahab's mistake and try to desperately avoid the same downfall in our own lives. We *must* let go of anything that hinders our faith. What we started when we accepted Christ as Savior, any progress we have made in our spiritual lives as we have walked with Christ, and even anything we have learned in this study will only last if we get rid of everything that hinders and anything that tries to pull us down.

God wants us to rid of any sin in our own lives. We can't change others, but we can pray for them, change any unhealthy habits we participate in with them, and then concentrate on ourselves. We have enough to deal with in our own lives and need not point fingers at anyone else for being the total cause of our problems. It is wise to make the right choices when we choose those with whom we associate. But regardless of what goes on around us, we can surely make changes in ourselves. Why? Because we want to know that our life pleases the Lord. We can *choose* to hear God's voice!

- **According to Hebrews 12:1, what are we to "throw off"? Then what are we to do?**

  _____

  _____

- **What things can easily entangle us?**

  _____

  _____

When we let God remove anything that hinders our walk with Him, we remove anything that may be blocking our ears from hearing His voice. It may be temporarily painful but worth it for the good of our spiritual health.

My son, Matthew, came to me crying with a splinter in his foot but would not let me pull it out. How often do we complain to God about our situation, but then do not let Him touch the real issue? We protect it—afraid it might hurt when He removes it. But then we spend our days limping around while it festers. Our Heavenly Father does not want to watch us limp through life, dragging our baggage behind us. Instead He wants us to trust Him with our lives and let Him gently remove what hurts us.

- Spend some time now with the Lord and ask Him to show you anything that may be hindering your walk with Him. Ask Him to help you make the appropriate changes in your life. Then ask God to give you a peace in your heart to know that you are living a life that is pleasing to Him.

Let's throw off everything that hinders . . . and run the race with victory!

NABOTH'S VINEYARD

WARMING UP

- Begin today by asking the Holy Spirit to speak to you through His Word.
- Please read 1 Kings 21:1-29.

ACT 6, SCENE 2

Do you ever experience an almost maddening reaction when you see something on television, read about an event, or hear a story about someone who has been treated unfairly? Don't you want to do something about it? Few things make my blood boil quicker than injustice. When the innocent are treated unfairly, I want God to intervene, free the oppressed, and bring justice. I shudder at what takes place in this world and I cry for the underdog. But these things do not go unnoticed by God and we will witness in our story today that He draws the line at inhumanity. So if these things break your heart too, then grab a few tissues and get ready to step up on your soapbox, because this is one of those kinds of stories.

THE SET:

Evidently King Ahab and Jezebel had a summer home in Jezreel.[31] There is nothing wrong with having more than one residence. If you do, feel free to invite me anytime! The breakdown in integrity and character happens when you have it all and you still want more. Ahab and Jezebel could be the stars of their own reality series called "What Not to Do." And little did he know it, but a Jezreelite named Naboth was about to be a guest on their show.

ENTER STAGE LEFT: NABOTH

Unfortunately for Naboth, he was at the right place at the wrong time. He owned a nice little piece of property, a vineyard that was near Ahab's palace in Jezreel (v. 1), and Ahab decided that he wanted it.

- **Have you ever been in the wrong place at the wrong time? If so, when?**

_____

_____

I know I have. It was my son's fifth birthday and he wanted to go bowling and then eat at McDonald's. Before eating we needed to wash our hands and go to the bathroom after touching all those bowling balls, but when we got to McDonald's, the women's restroom was out of order. Desperate, I asked my husband to watch the door of the men's restroom while I ran in. I forgot that men have difficulty multitasking, so when our boys deferred his attention, he failed to see the gentleman who walked into the men's restroom while I was still in there. (Since I am doing the typing, I get to tell my version of the story.) So instead of telling the stranger that I was in the stall, I froze! I backed into the corner of the stall and tried to hide my girly-shoes so he wouldn't know I was there. Then I had to suffer through what seemed like an eternity until he left. Upon seeing the man exit the men's room, my husband realized that someone had been in there with me. He quickly peeked in the door and sheepishly said, "S-u-u-u-u-san, are you okay?" I was totally in the *wrong* place at the *wrong* time! Poor Naboth was in the right place, but Ahab was in the wrong mood!

BLOCKADE #2 to hearing God's voice:
DEAFNESS DUE TO GREED

- What does Ahab offer in exchange for Naboth's vineyard in verse 2?

  _____

  _____

  _____

- Why doesn't Naboth want to sell his vineyard to Ahab in verse 3?

  _____

  _____

  _____

A very high value was placed on the continuity of a family's tenure of its ancestral land.[32] Although Ahab's bid was not a bad offer, it was still Naboth's right to keep his land within the family. This land held his inheritance, his worth, his family memories, and many years of labor cultivating the vineyard. The only good reason I can see to move would be to get away from Ahab and Jezebel. They weren't very friendly neighbors and I doubt they ever brought over homemade cookies. Regretfully, it was a decision that cost Naboth his life.

- **Do you think Naboth should have moved? Why or why not?**

  _____

  _____

When Naboth would not sell his land, the New International Version describes Ahab as "sullen and angry" in verse 4; the Revised Standard Version says he is "resentful and sullen;" and the King James says, "heavy and displeased." Any way you slice it, Ahab was acting like a baby! Verse 4 says, "He lay on his bed sulking and refused to eat." It sounds like an old-fashioned temper tantrum to me! "The only thing worse than a spoiled, pouting child is a spoiled, pouting adult!"[33]

Ahab's actions are so ridiculous that they are almost funny. But we have all known adults who pitch a fit and make a scene when they don't get their way, and it's not pretty. We don't let our kids act that way and get away with it, so why can adults? Eventually our actions, good or bad, will catch up with us. Choosing good over evil will end in a harvest of righteousness, but unchecked attitudes and actions end in destruction. Ahab's unchecked attitudes ended in destruction because they ended up in the hands of Jezebel.

EXIT: JEZEBEL (verses 5-23):

- Read verses 5-14 again. In a couple sentences, describe what happened.

_____

_____

_____

You don't have to be a sleuth to figure this one out. Jezebel took matters into her own spiny hands and got what she wanted—no matter the cost! The chilling fact of this story is her lack of conscience. Can we say "pathological"? Whew! She was a nutcase! I truly believe Jezebel thought she answered to no one. She was without conscience and without God. But everyone will go before God one day and stand accountable for their actions. Please read Revelation 2:20-23.

- **For what is the name "Jezebel" used as synonym?**

_____

_____

- **In 1 Kings 21:23, what will become of Jezebel?**

_____

- Now look at 2 Kings 9:30-37. Was his prophecy about Jezebel fulfilled just as Elijah said?

_____

This act of murderous disobedience and greed was the last straw for God's patience. Jezebel dug her own grave to a painful and humiliating end. Let's go ahead and say a happy goodbye to Jezebel. It does not seem like a moment too soon. We have seen enough!

RE-ENTER: ELIJAH (verses 17-26)

After not hearing from Elijah in a little while, he reappears on the scene as God's chosen messenger. Ahab greets Elijah in his usual twisted way, saying, "So you have found me, my enemy!" (v. 20). But Ahab's true enemy is himself, not Elijah.

- How is Ahab described in verses 25 and 26?

- What will happen to Ahab when he dies? (verse 19)

_____

- What will happen to all of Ahab's descendants? (verse 21)

_____

GOD'S JUDGEMENT (verse 27):

I don't always understand why evildoers seem to get away with their behavior for so long. I know this is a fallen world, so we are all victims of the choices that others make. But it just doesn't seem fair, does it? If I could sit down with God and ask Him a question that He would audibly answer, it would be this one: "Why are innocent people allowed to suffer at the hands of evildoers?" But

I am comforted to know that God does not tolerate injustice. The Lord drew the eternal line with Jezebel and it's Ahab's turn to come face-to-face with the God of justice!

- In verse 27, what was Ahab's reaction to God's verdict?

_____

_____

GOD'S MERCY (verses 28-29):

Unlike Jezebel, I guess Ahab had a conscience. But was it too little too late?

- Do you ever feel like you have messed up one too many times for God to forgive you? Has anyone wronged you one too many times to forgive?

_____

_____

- **Fill in the blanks below to see how God handled Ahab's repentance in verses 28-29. "Then the word of the Lord came to Elijah the Tishbite: 'Have you noticed how Ahab has _____ himself before me? Because he has _____ himself, I will _____ bring this disaster _____ _____ _____, but I will bring it on his house in the days _____ _____ _____.'"**
- **What is your reaction to God's decision?**

_____

_____

God shows Ahab mercy by posting his bail for a little while and leaving him to do a little more community service. Ahab's repentance and humility were pleasing to God, and it bought Ahab a little more time. Nothing is recorded about Ahab's children serving the Lord. In fact, 1 Kings 22:52 states that their son, Ahaziah, "did evil in the eyes of the LORD, because he walked in the ways of his father and mother." So don't cry for him! In fact, God extended His mercy to the whole motley crew and gave them all another chance. God is all-loving, merciful, and just, so we can trust that He knows what is right.

Praise the Lord, with God it is never too late! God is just and merciful at the same time. Only the Almighty Judge can be so wise and so loving. I love Exodus 34:6-7. Turn with me to this passage of Scripture, which is perhaps one of the most beautiful verses in the Bible, when God chose to reveal himself to Moses, and *to us*, through His own autobiography.

- How does God describe Himself and His motives in Exodus 34:6?

_____

_____

_____

- How does He deal with those who are repentant in verse 7?

_____

- How does He deal with the guilty?

_____

God is compassionate, gracious, loving, and faithful. He is forgiving and just at the same time. We can trust Him with the issues of life that do not seem to make any sense. He is in control! He is good! And He is loving toward all He has made! When we are tempted to worry that God does not seem to care about the injustice around us, let us be reminded: that is precisely why He sent Jesus to this earth! Jesus proclaimed that He was sent to "preach good news to the poor . . . proclaim freedom for the prisoners . . . give recovery of sight for the blind . . . to release the oppressed . . ." (Luke 4:18).

Ahab was the recipient of God's grace. God never gives up on us, either. I may never understand it, but I will forever be grateful. We are all sinners, just like Ahab. And believe it or not, when we mess up . . . we should act like Ahab. *Just this once.*

PRIDE BEFORE THE FALL

WARMING UP

- Begin today by asking the Holy Spirit to speak to you through His Word.
- Please read 1 Kings 22:1-40.

ACT 6, SCENE 3

I am sad to see our time together almost come to an end, but don't EXIT just yet. We have a couple more stops to make before the dramatic conclusion to Elijah's story. In today's scripture we have skipped forward three years to view this scene between Ahab, king of Israel, and Jehoshaphat, king of Judah.

ENTER: King Jehoshaphat

This same scene is also recorded in 2 Chronicles 18 and adds the fact that King Jehoshaphat had allied himself with King Ahab by marriage. Well now, wasn't that convenient?! So for now, there is peace between Israel and Judah and things have also been quiet between Israel and its enemy, Aram, for at least three years. But Aram still held Ramoth Gilead (the city on the northeast side of the Jordan River hugging the border between Israel and Aram) in its possession even though it rightfully belonged to Israel (verses 1-3).

- **What did Jehoshaphat and Ahab decide to do in verse 4?**

  _____

  _____

- **What was Jehoshaphat's request in verse 5 before committing to help Israel fight their battle?**

  _____

  _____

Good advice. I like King Jehoshaphat. I wish Ahab had taken more cues from him. If he had, Ahab's lines in this script would have been a little more pleasant and his role would not have been cut from the story quite so soon. Ahab did decide to get counsel, but he took a shortcut *again* and found four hundred "prophets" that would tell him what he wanted to hear instead of the truth.

- In your own words, what did the prophets tell Ahab in response to his question, "Shall I go to war against Ramoth Gilead, or should I refrain?" (See verse 6)

  _____

  _____

There are so many teaching moments here, not the least of which is to be careful from whom you get advice. It may be easier to handpick our favorite people who always make us feel good, but they may not always be doing us *much* good! Only advice that agrees with God's Word is reliable.

I just love God's Word. Not only are matchless truths found there, but also many entertaining tales filled with humor. This is one chapter that has both. So, now for the funny part . . . Loosely translated, Jehoshaphat basically says to Ahab in verse 7, "No, really. Who else are you going to ask? You have *got* to be kidding!" Then Ahab says to Jehoshaphat, "There is yet one man by whom we may inquire of the LORD, Michaiah the son of Imlah, but I hate him, for he never prophesies good concerning me, but evil" (v. 8). There was a reason these true prophets of God never had anything good to say about Ahab . . . it was because there was nothing good to say about Ahab! After all Ahab has gone through, he will never grow up, will he?

- **Who in your life will tell you the truth *in love*? Are you willing to listen?**

_____

_____

ENTER: MICHAIAH, THE SON OF IMLAH

Micaiah's very name means "Who is like Yahweh?" and he lives up to his name of honor.[34] In Verse 14 Micaiah says, "As surely as the LORD lives, I can tell him only what the LORD tells me."

- Please read verses 14-17 again. Is anyone else here confused besides me? What do you think is going on?

_____

_____

Didn't Michaiah just say he would only speak the truth? I'm guessing that there was some other sarcastic body language going on here because Ahab seemed to know that Micaiah was joking. Ahab says to Micaiah, "How many times must I make you swear to tell me nothing but the truth in the name of the LORD?" Oh, so *now* Ahab wants the truth. I don't think he can handle the truth!

BLOCKADE #3 to hearing God's voice:
DEAFNESS DUE TO PRIDE

Ahab has given us many examples of pride in these pages of his life. He was nothing short of an evil, overgrown crybaby. But I believe each one of his problems was rooted in pride. He allowed anyone who got in his way to be killed. He sulked and threw fits when his authority was questioned. He worshipped Baal and set up altars and Asherah poles so he could rule his own life instead of obeying God. That's pride. Pride became the blockade that kept Ahab from hearing and obeying God's voice.

Unfortunately, I can identify with Ahab again. When Brent and I were newlyweds, we loved to play golf together. The only problem was that I was a beginner and he had been playing for years.

So I took a few lessons, played a few nine-hole courses very badly, and then we left for vacation with his family. I was so gung ho about learning to play golf that I decided to play with the men in our family instead of kicking back on the beach with the girls. (I have come to my senses since then!) But it became a favorite family story because of my choice . . .

I still could barely achieve liftoff with my ball, much less keep up with the guys for eighteen holes. By the ninth hole I had bloodied my hands so badly that bandages across my palms were not enough to cover my broken blisters. So I wore a golf glove on both hands and kept playing. I had a sunburn, bumped my head on the golf cart, and accidentally rammed my father-in-law's golf cart in front of me when I hit the gas instead of the brakes. My pride not only hurt myself, but I took others down with me. I quickly became infamous in the family for being very hardheaded when it came to knowing when to quit!

Pride before the fall!

EXIT: King Ahab

- **Now let's take a sneak peek into heaven as we read this next portion of the scripture. It is a little unsettling. Read verses 19-23. What did God do and what is your reaction?**

  _____

  _____

  _____

It may seem odd that God would use a lying spirit to entice Ahab, but the Lord had warned Ahab that his idolatrous living and evil ways would end in death. In fact, God had already given Ahab many chances to repent, yet Ahab refused to change. In yesterday's lesson we witnessed the beautiful grace of God as He showed mercy on a repentant Ahab. But, unfortunately, Ahab once again chose to block the voice of God in his life. This time the result was not only *deafness* to God's voice, but also *death*.

God had been more than patient and merciful with Ahab, but enough was enough. Pride had deafened his ears to hear truth, and so pride was a fitting way for God to lure Ahab into the battle that would end his life.

- **What happened to Ahab's blood in verse 38? Where was his chariot washed?**

  _____

- How is this scene a fitting conclusion to Ahab's life considering chapter 21:25 says he "sold himself" to do evil in the eyes of the Lord?

  _____

GOODBYE, AHAB!

But before we get too cocky, we would be wise to take a difficult look in the mirror. The sin of pride is easy to overlook. It is not always as blatant as Ahab's sin. Pride can also be a quiet, private sin. We might be tempted to sweep those kinds of little quirks about ourselves under the rug. We might tell ourselves that no one else will be affected. Obviously, this is not true. The result of pride is devastating for all of us. Pride can creep in if we try to get the credit for our achievements, if we think we are better than someone else who messes up, or if we think our success is our own doing. There is nothing wrong with some of those things. Success, serving, and self-confidence are fine . . . unless we feel like they have anything at to do with us. At that point they become destructive.

- **What other ways can pride creep into our lives?**

_____

_____

Thank you for working so hard and allowing God to speak to every part of your life—no matter how uncomfortable that may be. The results are not only eternal, but also life-changing, even now! In tomorrow's lesson we will find the antidote for this blockade to hearing God's voice. God has been speaking to me and I pray that He has been revealing Himself to you as well. But, thank God, He is not finished with us yet! Let's prepare our hearts to receive all God has in store for us tomorrow as we seek His refining work in our lives. Expect great things!

"Consecrate yourselves, for tomorrow the LORD will do amazing things among you" (Josh. 3:5).

ACTING THE PART

WARMING UP

- Begin today by asking the Holy Spirit to speak to you through His Word.
- Please read 2 Kings 1:1-18.

ACT 6, SCENE 4

Yesterday we said goodbye to Ahab, but there's a new kid in town—Ahab and Jezebel's kid—and unfortunately, he gets to be king. Even more unfortunate is the fact that he lived his life every bit as evil as his parents.

ENTER STAGE RIGHT: AHAZIAH

- Please read 1 Kings 22:51-53. List all the ways that Ahaziah provoked the Lord to anger.

_____

_____

_____

The bad apple doesn't fall far from the rotten tree, does it? Knowing the high price Ahab and Jezebel paid for their sins, Ahaziah should have avoided the same demise at all costs. But I guess being hardheaded ran in the family as much as pride, selfishness, and a general un-likeability. The scene opens in our story today with Ahaziah falling through a lattice in his house. He is unable to recover from his fall and sends messengers to inquire of Baal-zebub if he will regain his health.

RE-ENTER: ELIJAH

- **In verse 3, what question does the angel of the Lord tell Elijah to ask Ahaziah?**

_____

_____

- Therefore, what is Ahaziah's fate in verse 4?

_____

_____

BLOCKADE #4 to hearing God's voice:
DEAFNESS DUE TO SELFISHNESS

Ahaziah was unwilling to seek the voice of the Lord in his situation; instead, he asked for the opinion of Baal-zebub. He did not want God to be his god. Call it "strongholds," "addictions," "hang-ups," "habits," or "weaknesses"—but any way you look at it, you can define the roots of these sins as our selfish attempts to be our own god. When we try to find our own way to fill our voids and build confidence in ourselves, we are trapped. Ahaziah was trapped in an outward illness that mirrored his sick heart. It was a disease that he could not shake as long as he was unwilling to let go of his pride like his father, Ahab. And so, it would become his terminal illness.

Nobody sets out with the intent of becoming selfish and prideful, but it's easy to find ourselves fighting the same battles with pride over and over. It takes more than minor surgery to avoid and overcome pride in our lives before it eats us alive. But the alternative could lead to the death of what is most precious to us: our relationship with God and our ability to hear His still, small voice in our lives. It is worth it to get to the root of the problem, my friend. A life of freedom, joy, and a personal relationship with God is our great reward! (See Genesis 15:1.)

- What do you think is the antidote to selfishness?

_____

_____

A Slice of Humble Pie

It is important to recognize the difference between poor self-esteem and humility. I have heard it said that humility is not thinking less of your self, but simply thinking of yourself less. Pride, on the other hand, is the attempt to prove our self-worth to others, to ourselves, and even to God. Then *self* becomes the focus and the problem.

- List a word(s) that you think is the opposite of each of these types of pride:

Self-ambition

_____

Greed

_____

Coveting

_____

Selfishness

_____

Attention-seeking

_____

Adultery

_____

Conceit

_____

Has to be my way

_____

What a great idea . . . but how do we do it? How do we shake off the desire to do things our way? How do we get *humble*? Let's look at two ways we can pride-proof our lives and gain unselfish humility.

1. CONFESSION:

Ahaziah did not want to know God's opinion of the state he was in because he did not want to confess his sin. He wanted to continue his sinful way of life and still get the blessing. Those two things are like polar opposites of a magnet, like mixing oil and water, like an Alabama fan living with an Auburn fan (oh, sorry, those are my issues)—it cannot happen. God will not bless us when we are in sin. *But God is anxious to meet us where we are.*

When we humble ourselves before God through confession, it is like cleaning off the windshield of our souls. I have a friend who likes to say that when she stands in God's presence, it is like looking through a windshield that seems clear enough to her at first glance, but when the sun shines through it, all the dirt shows up. It is an act of humility to admit our weaknesses. We may be tempted to try to get cleaned up by ourselves, but that doesn't get the job done. The dirt is still there. It would be silly to try to look perfect before we approach God, just as it would be silly to clean the house before the maid comes (if we are lucky)! If we approach God daily with an attitude of humility, we allow Him to clean off the grime that so easily builds up in our lives. Then we are able to see Him and hear His voice more clearly in our lives. It is God's job to cleanse our souls, but we must be willing to show Him our mess.

- Are you willing to show God your "mess" or do you want to get cleaned up before you approach Him?

- Will you humble yourself right now and ask the Lord what He sees in your life?
- After confessing our sin, what do we have through our Lord Jesus Christ according to Romans 5:1?

The second step for *pride-proofing* our lives and gaining an unselfish humility is . . .

2. PRAISE:

God always gets my attention through my children. When our youngest son, John David, was about two-and-a-half years old, we had suffered through a very dry summer in Oklahoma. There were rations placed on all homes for limited water usage, our yard looked as dry as the wheat farms nearby, and the heat zapped our energy to do much activity or recreation. Finally it began to sprinkle some rain three months later. I will never forget John David's little voice chattering behind me from his car seat as we watched the raindrops cut through the dust on our windshield. I couldn't understand what he said, so I asked him, "What did you say, John David?" He replied loud and clear, "I pwaising!" He still had trouble pronouncing his "r's," so I asked again, "You said you are praying?" Then he replied, "No. I pwaising for the wain!"

We may not always feel like praising in the midst of tough times, but we must look for the little sprinkles of His faithfulness around us. God doesn't just deserve our praise when He answers our prayers. God is always faithful and good. May we never be guilty of holding back from freely worshipping God and "pwaising" Him with all our might, regardless of our situation. We may be the inspiration someone needs to feel free to praise God with abandon. We may be the reminder someone needs that God is faithful no matter what circumstances arise.

This is how we develop a humility that pleases God. Humility comes when we know that our next breath is given to us only by the grace of God; when we know that every good thing we have is given from the goodness of God; when we know that any talents, accomplishments or qualities worth being proud of are gifts from God; when we *choose* to praise no matter our situation because God is worthy all the time.

- **Read Psalms. 42:11. What does this Psalm mean to you in your current situation?**

_____

_____

Then there are other times when we praise because our cup overflows with thanksgivings and gratitude. At times like these, we can't not praise! If we don't praise, it seems we will burst! Not long ago I was experiencing a moment like this while driving and singing praise music in my car. I felt God's presence so close and I was overcome by His love and goodness to me. I felt like putting a bumper sticker on my car that said, "Praise or Bust!" I was already singing to the top of my voice (probably to the amusement of passersby), but I was having a hard time raising my hands while driving, so I stopped and wrote these words:

> *Because of what God has done for me,*
>
> *I will speak His name for all to hear.*
>
> *But if I cannot speak, I will dance.*
>
> *If I cannot dance, I will sing.*
>
> *If I cannot sing . . . I will lift my hands.*
>
> *Because my soul must praise!*

I have been looking forward to writing this part of our study ever since God first spoke to me from the pages of 1 and 2 Kings. We came into our study with open hearts to all God had in store for us and we are going to go out in praise for His faithfulness to speak to us! God's Word has been a healing balm to our every point of need as we have walked alongside Elijah during his ministry. How could we do anything except praise?! God has been faithful and good, loving and forgiving, challenging and rewarding, inspiring and changing. Does anyone else besides me want to throw your hands up and shout, "HALLELUJAH!"?

- **What has God done for you during this study of His Word? Write a prayer of praise and thanksgiving for Who He is and what He has done for you.**

_____

_____

_____

Let's lift our eyes to our salvation and lift our voices together in praise. We are recipients of God's grace—so let's act like it! Sing, speak, dance, or lift your hands, child of God, but don't hold back! *Because you were made to praise!*

CURTAIN CALL

WARMING UP

- Begin today by asking the Holy Spirit to speak to you through His Word.
- Please read 2 Kings 2:1-14.

ACT 6, SCENE 5

Can this really be our last day? This final day of our study together is bittersweet for me. I am sad for our time together to end because it has been an incredible blessing to walk beside you on this journey through Scripture. I am also sad to say goodbye to Elijah—a seemingly old friend after we have followed every scene of his life over the last six weeks.

But I am excited at the same time about the conclusion of our study because it marks a new beginning. Where this breathtaking finale to the story of Elijah ends, the sequel to the story begins in our lives. I am already on the edge of my seat, ready to witness one of the most spectacular exits from the stage of this earthly realm that any human being has ever experienced. Get your popcorn in hand and join me one last time as the curtain rises to reveal the final scene.

ELIJAH'S FINAL SCENE

ENTER TOGETHER: ELISHA and ELIJAH

Well, we are not alone as we anticipate the going home party for Elijah. Someone else is just as sad to see his dear friend exit the stage. Elisha has been walking in the footprints of Elijah for some time now. He has been a most studious understudy, readying himself for the day when he must take the proverbial prophet-baton from Elijah. But Elisha is not champing at the bit. He knows what it takes to walk a mile in Elijah's sandals, and he knows what a gift it has been to have had such a tremendous teacher and friend.

As Elisha reappears on the set in this portion of Scripture, he seems well aware of God's plan to take Elijah from him that very day.

- Look at 2 Kings 2:1. Where are Elijah and Elisha at this time?
  _____

- **Now read verse 2. What is Elijah's command for Elisha?**
  _____

- **Does this idea sit well with Elisha? _____. What is his reply in verses 2, 4, and 6?**
  _____
  _____

THE SET:

The set is going to change rapidly today. The Lord moves Elijah around quite a bit before his grand finale. The starting point for Elijah and Elisha is Gilgal, which is approximately ten miles north of the Dead Sea. From there they traveled to Bethel, which is about fifteen miles west of Gilgal.

- Where did Elijah go next according to verse 4?

  _____

- And then where did he go, as recorded in verse 6?

  _____

- **What happened each time Elijah and Elisha arrived at their new destination in verses 3 and 5? Who was waiting for them and what did they know?**

  _____

  _____

- In your own words, what was Elisha's response to the comments made by the company of prophets each time they arrived at their new destination?

  _____

  _____

News traveled more quickly in Israel than gossip through the church grapevine! They had no prayer chains or text messaging or Facebook—just the information superhighway of the Holy Spirit. Pretty impressive networking. This company of prophets was apparently "a band or group of persons called to the prophetic ministry who studied and learned under the great prophet figures, such as Samuel, Elijah, Elisha, Isaiah, and others"[35]Basically, these schools were like ancient seminaries, and these students were privileged enough to witness the succession of ministry from Elijah to Elisha. But Elisha did not seem to care for what these students had to say. Elisha was not happy that Elijah was leaving. In fact, he never left Elijah's side during the last few moments of Elijah's life; and for good reason. Elisha wanted something that Elijah had.

EXIT: ELIJAH

Distribution of the Holy Spirit to Elisha:

- **What did Elisha ask Elijah to give him in verse 9?**

  _____

In the Old Testament, the Holy Spirit was given only to certain people at certain times for certain tasks. The wording used in verse 9 is of great significance. Elisha asked to "inherit" a "double portion" (NIV) or "double share" (RSV) of the Spirit that God had given Elijah. The purpose for the word "inherit" comes from Deuteronomy 21:15-17. Here it is explained that the eldest son is entitled to inherit a "double share" of the inheritance when his father died. Elisha literally sees himself as Elijah's firstborn successor to Elijah's prophetic ministry.

- What did Elisha call Elijah as he was taken up to heaven in verse 12?

  _____

When Elisha makes his request, he does not ask for the typical inheritance of land or possessions; instead, he asks for a double portion of Elijah's spirit. The Hebrew translations of these words are very interesting. The word *double* is translated from the word *shenayim* (shen-ah'-yim), meaning "second, again, another." The word *portion* comes from the Hebrew word *peh*, meaning "the mouth, as the means of blowing." And *Spirit* comes from *r^uwach* (roo-akh), which means "wind, breath, exhalation."[36] When you put the meaning of these words together, Elisha was very literally asking for God to breathe with His mouth His Spirit onto him, just as God had done for Elijah. In other words, "Do it again, Lord. For me!"

- **In verse 10, what did Elijah say the criteria would be for Elisha to know he had received his request?**

  _____

  _____

- **Look at verse 11-12. What did Elisha see?**

  _____

- **In verse 13, what was the visual reminder and source of power left behind for Elisha?**

  _____

  _____

God left behind Elijah's cloak (NIV) or mantle (RSV) for Elisha. As you may recall, Elijah's cloak was used as part of Elisha's call in 1 Kings 19. And now God uses Elijah's cloak as a symbol of the *fulfillment* of that call. To me, that is so exciting! Because it shows that God does not ask us to serve Him unprepared. He equips us first. God gave Elisha a period of time to train for his ministry. Now he is ready to serve on his own. Elijah's cloak, once used for mentoring, is now given as power to fulfill his call.

I love this statement from the *Beacon Bible Commentary*: "Elijah's mantle fell where Elisha could pick it up. The availability of the mantle authenticated Elisha's receipt of the 'double portion.' It was, in effect, God's further endorsement of him as Elijah's successor and a symbol that God's power would rest on him as it had on Elijah."[37]

Elisha saw. He received. Then he went.

Beautifully, we have been given the chance to do the same. It is time for our curtain call. Instead of sitting on the front row observing, it is our turn to step onto the stage. The sequel to Elijah's story is our story.

CURTAIN CALL

Distribution of the Holy Spirit to us:

After the death and resurrection of Jesus Christ, we were promised the coming of the Holy Spirit for those who believe in Jesus's name. (See Luke 24:49.)

- How was that promise fulfilled in Acts 2:1-4?

  _____

  _____

- **What promise is given in Acts 2:17 regarding us?**

  _____

  _____

Do you know what that means, my friend? That means we have seen His glory! We have been witnesses of the resurrection of Jesus in God's Word. Then we receive His Spirit when we accept Christ as our personal Savior. The presence and the power of God is ours for the asking! Just as Elisha asked Elijah for a double portion of his spirit, we can ask to inherit all God has for us! I can't write this paragraph without using lots of exclamation points! It's just too exciting!!!

- **How does this make you feel? Are you encouraged? Nervous? Champing at the bit to get going?**

  _____

  _____

- God has promised you that His Holy Spirit will be with you always (Matthew 28:20). Ask God to fill you with His Holy Spirit and give you power from on high. Then write a prayer of response to the Lord, thanking Him for His faithfulness and asking Him to help you continue to seek His voice and obediently follow where He leads:

  _____

  _____

  _____

You have seen. You have received. Now it is time to go!

You have a role to play in God's kingdom that was written especially for you. Thank the Lord because He will not send you out unequipped. Allow the Lord the chance to prepare you. Continue to seek out godly mentors to help you along your journey. Wait on the Lord. Continue educating yourself in your area of involvement. But, most of all, continue to seek God's voice! Nothing can compare to the personal guidance, inspiration, and power of the Holy Spirit as you answer His call on your life.

All of the PREP STEPS that you practice each day are not just a means to an end. They are not just used to go through the motions. Meditating on God's Word, praying, being still, and responding with obedience are more than a formula to follow. *It is about a relationship.* Yes, God has called you for a special purpose, but the role God asks you to play will undoubtedly change over time. *What* you do is not nearly as important to Him as doing it *with* Him. At the end of your life, the most wonderful parts of your story will not be what you accomplished for God, but your crowning moments of joy will be the moments when you heard the still, small voice of your Master as he very personally led you through every new ACT and SCENE of your life.

Until that day when the Lord sweeps you up in His Spirit and calls you home, seek Him with all your heart. The gentle whispers of God are the best part of this life!

So listen closely . . . *He is calling!*

DIRECTOR'S NOTES

This book is designed as a six-week Bible study that can be done as individual devotionals or as a group. The most effective plan is to do a lesson five days a week and then meet together as a group once a week to discuss insights from the daily lessons. The small group leader can follow the plan below for convenience:

1. Pick a time and place to meet.
2. Delegate someone to plan refreshments.
3. Make sure everyone registered has a workbook. (An NIV Bible would also be helpful.)
4. Session components: (Each session is designed to last approximately sixty minutes.)
   - Begin with snacks and fellowship for the first five to ten minutes.
   - Send a prayer request list around the room while eating for anyone that feels comfortable sharing their requests.
   - Open with prayer and ask the Holy Spirit to guide your conversations for His glory and to give you His Spirit of revelation and understanding.
   - Discuss the questions in **bold print** from each day's lessons. It may be helpful to read a few sentences just before the discussion question to get everyone on the same page. There are usually two or three questions per lesson. So ask participants to keep the answers brief so that everyone who wishes to respond is able to do so.
   - Close with a time of prayer for the written requests and if anyone needs special prayer after the discussions. The leader can pray each week or you may want to ask someone AHEAD OF TIME from the group to close in prayer. Never surprise someone by asking them to pray in front of others. That terrifies some people. Another effective way to pray for each other is to have a time of silent prayer for the person on your left and then the person on your right.
   - Check my website, **susanvanhook.com**, for any DVD sessions that you may want to add to your small group meetings. A DVD lesson will add about fifteen extra minutes to your time together. These video sessions will follow your discussion of the previous week's lessons and add valuable inspiration and insight to the upcoming week.

As leader of your group, always be sure to pray for God to speak to you personally, allowing His Word to apply to your own life before you ask the same of others in your group. Pray for the Lord to speak to your group during your sessions. Then pray for each member of your small group to individually experience God in a special way. I am praying for you and your group as you encounter the life-changing Word of God. Expect great things from our wonderful Lord! For He "is able to do immeasurably more than all we ask or imagine, according to his power that is at work within us" (Eph. 3:20a). To God be the glory!

ABOUT THE AUTHOR

Susan Michelle Van Hook's first loves will always be the Lord Jesus, her husband, and her children. But she is also passionate about her role as teacher of God's Word to others. No stranger to the ministry, she was born as a MK (Missionary's kid) in Montego Bay, Jamaica, where her parents were missionaries. When they moved back to Huntsville, Alabama, she became a PK (preacher's kid). She is now a PW (preacher's wife) and a PKM (preacher's kid's mom). She has always had her own personal relationship with Jesus Christ and enjoys serving His church. But it wasn't until she plunged deeply into God's Word as an adult that God began to call her personally to the ministry—and instilled within her a vibrant passion for teaching God's Word. Her desire is for everyone to experience God's voice in the midst of everyday life because it changes everything! She wants God's Word to bring encouragement in the midst of chaos because that is where God usually speaks to her—somewhere between making a peanut butter and jelly sandwich and a trip to the dry cleaners.

Susan Michelle graduated from Trevecca Nazarene University in Nashville, Tennessee, as a Physician Assistant. She currently lives in Wichita, Kansas, with her husband, Brent, the senior pastor of Wichita First Church of the Nazarene; their two sons, Matthew and John David; and beloved Labradoodle, Sneaker. Susan serves God through writing, speaking, teaching Sunday school, singing in her church choir, and as director of Living Waters Compassionate Ministries.

CREDITS

Act 1

1. *Life Application Bible, NIV* (Wheaton, IL: Tyndale House Publishing, Inc., 1988, 1989, 1990, 1991), 580.

2. Ibid.

3. Ibid., 583.

4. Ibid., 747.

5. *Oxford Dictionary and Thesaurus* (New York, NY: Oxford University Press, Inc., 2002, 2008).

Act 2

6. This is a true story, but the names have been changed for protection of the individuals in the story.

7. Harvey E. Finley, *Beacon Hill Commentary* (Kansas City, MO: Beacon Hill Press, 1965), 421.

8. Gary A. Haugen, *Just Courage* (Downers Grove, IL: InterVarsity Press, 2008), 108.

9. Ibid., 77.

10. Henry T. Blackaby and Claude V. King, *Experiencing God* (Nashville, TN: LifeWay Press, 1990), 66.

Act 3

11. *Strong's Concordance* (Nashville, TN: Thomas Nelson Publishers, 1990).

12. Henry and Richard Blackaby, *Hearing God's Voice* (Nashville, TN: Broadman and Holman Publishers, Inc., 2002), 133.

13. Anne Graham Lotz, *The Magnificent Obsession* (Grand Rapids, MI: Zondervan, 2009), 146.

14. Richard J. Foster, *Celebration Of Discipline* (New York, NY: Harper Collins Publishers, 1978, 1988), 40.

15. Ibid., 35.

16. *Strong's Concordance* (Nashville, TN: Thomas Nelson Publishers, 1990).

17. Henry T. and Richard Blackaby, *Hearing God's Voice* (Nashville, TN: Broadman and Holman Publishers, 2002), 123.

Act 4

18. Ibid., 31.

19. Ibid., 91

20. Ibid., 190.

21. Laurie Beth Jones, *Jesus Life Coach Journal* (Nashville, TN: Thomas Nelson Book Group, 2004), 16.

22. Richard J. Foster, *Celebration Of Discipline* (New York, NY: Harper Collins Publishers, 1978, 1988), 27.

23. A. Graeme Auld, *The Daily Study Bible Series: 1 & 2 Kings* (Edinburgh, Scotland: The Saint Andrew Press and Philadelphia, PN: The Westminster Press, 1986), pgs. 122-123.

24. Richard J. Foster, *Celebration Of Discipline* (New York, NY: Harper Collins Publishers, 1978, 1988), 23.

25. Henry T. and Richard Blackaby, *Hearing God's Voice* (Nashville, TN: Broadman and Holman Publishers, 2002), 107.

26. Beth Moore, *Believing God Devotional Journal* (Nashville, TN: Broadman and Holman Publishers, Inc., 2004), 18.

Act 5

27. Daniel M. Hyde, *United Methodist Churches Newsletter to Boonesville, Harms, and Mulberry, TN., March 2009.*

28. *Strong's Concordance* (Nashville, TN: Thomas Nelson Publishers, 1990).

29. Harvey E. Finley, *Beacon Bible Commentary* (Kansas City, MO: Beacon Hill Press, 1965), 426.

Act 6

30. *The Life Application Bible, NIV* (Wheaton, IL: Tyndale House Publishers, Inc., 1988, 1989, 1990, 1991), 587.

31. Harvey E. Finley, *Beacon Bible Commentary* (Kansas City, MO: Beacon Hill Press, 1965), 431.

32. A. Graeme Auld, *The Daily Study Bible Series: 1 & 2 Kings* (Edinburgh, Scotland: The Saint Andrew Press and Philadelphia, PN: The Westminster Press, 1986), 136.

33. Harvey E. Finley, *Beacon Bible Commentary* (Kansas City, MO: Beacon Hill Press, 1965), 431.

34. A. Graeme Auld, *The Daily Study Bible Series: 1 & 2 Kings* (Edinburgh, Scotland: The Saint Andrew Press and Philadelphia, PN: The Westminster Press, 1986), 143.

35. Harvey E. Finley, *Beacon Bible Commentary* (Kansas City, MO: Beacon Hill Press, 1965), 441.

36. *Strong's Concordance* (Nashville, TN: Thomas Nelson Publishers, 1990).

37. Harvey E. Finley, Beacon Bible Commentary (Kansas City, MO: Beacon Hill Press, 1965), 439.